My INCREDIBLE JOURNEY

From Cadet to Command

My INCREDIBLE JOURNEY

From Cadet to Command

Rear Admiral
Peter Dingemans

BREWIN BOOKS

First published by
Brewin Books Ltd, 56 Alcester Road,
Studley, Warwickshire B80 7LG in 2013
www.brewinbooks.com

ISBN: 978-1-85858-501-7

A Cataloguing in Publication Record
for this title is available from the British Library

Typeset in Minion Pro
Printed in Great Britain by
Berforts Information Press.

CONTENTS

ACKNOWLEDGEMENTS

Along the way a great many people have offered help and advice, taken time to read the book and offer both friendly and professional help.

I would like to thank Derek Parsons who lent me his diary which not only inspired me to write the book, but reminded me of the time and dates of many events.

Thanks to Jonathan Lloyd of Curtis Brown who kindly gave me advice and encouragement.

Sir Lionel Freedman who allowed me to use quotes from his book and thanks to Dr Anthony Seldon for reading it and offering helpful advice.

Professor Keith Middlemass I offer many thanks for your suggestions and professional expertise which was very much appreciated.

David Dobson who pointed me in many right directions to people of influence.

Clive Jeffries thank you we have come a long way since our first meeting, thank you for the trouble you took with the book.

Bob Lane gave a huge amount of support and contributions to the book including the best description of de-ballasting I have ever read, many thanks to you. Thanks to all the intrepid crew members who let me put their stories in the book.

Martin Griffiths for reading a first draft and offering help and advice and David Joel Captain of Woolaston who checked and added events to the Woolaston chapter many thanks to you both.

Malcolm McCleod whose invaluable help knocked the Falklands chapter into shape.

Bruce Webb who was and continues to be a wonderful source of strength to me just as he was in the Falklands Conflict as my navigator. A real unsung hero.

Thanks to Maggie Koumi for the very conscientious work she did dotting i's, crossing t's, tidying up the prose, and providing an editorial overview. Thanks to my sister Joanna who transcribed my tapes, downloaded my pictures and shouted at me when I didn't send the right tapes, but brought all the bits and pieces together to create the book. Without Joanna this book could not have been produced.

Thanks to my sons Timothy, James and Piers for making me a very proud father and grandfather. Finally thanks to my very dear wife Faith for everything, she has supported me throughout my career, and again over the last three years as I have attempted to write about my career. She has put up with endless computer problems and being inundated with reams of paper, as I photostat and print endless copies of my prose and pictures.

There are many people who I have left out of the thanks and I apologise if I have failed to mention you, but you know who you are so thank you.

FOREWORD

Foreword by Admiral Sir Mark Stanhope
GCB OBE ADC, First Sea Lord and Chief of Naval Staff

I have always believed that the art of leadership is about inspiring others to aspire. Leadership brings meaning to what we do because leadership helps those we lead make the connection between *why* we do things and *how* we do things. In other words, leaders provide purpose.

Rear Admiral Peter Dingemans' unique and incredible journey provides the reader with a very personal account of how he learned his art of leadership and, perhaps more importantly, how he put it into practice by tailoring it to the nuance of the moment. In staff appointments and sea commands, in times of routine and times of change, and in peace and war, such rich seams of experience, exposed through a combination of poignant vignettes and light anecdotes, make this interesting and enjoyable reading.

As much as this is a book about the art of leadership, it is also about, as Peter puts it, "the art of being at sea". An art that he considers essential for all sailors and marines to learn and refine throughout their careers – just as he did himself. For the mariners amongst us, the need for an intuitive understanding of the sea will be obvious, but for those whose lives are based ashore, the book gives a helpful glimpse into the universal challenges of the world's most diverse environment. The sea: beguiling one minute, hostile the next.

This is also a book which reveals much about the enduring character of the Royal Navy's core values – of commitment, courage, discipline, respect for others, integrity and loyalty. Collectively they contribute to the Royal Navy's organisational culture or, to put it in the vernacular, our ethos. An ethos that serves as the glue that ensures the bonds between us are ever-present and ever-strong.

And yet I would suggest that our ethos is more than that. As this book reminds us, our ethos helps 'pre-load' our loyal Service men and women with an all-important instinctive moral response. Necessarily instinctive because the complex and rapidly changing battle space of modern warfare and crisis engagement bombards sailors and marines with a wealth of information, often requiring them to make important decisions immediately, and much lower down the rank structure and command chain. So with that embedded ethos, our people can respond swiftly with a moral confidence, as they did during the Falklands Conflict, and as our sailors and marines do today when they board a pirate vessel in the Indian Ocean or when they patrol the streets of Helmand in Afghanistan.

In particular though, it is Peter's recollection of his time in command of HMS INTREPID (for the second occasion) during the Falklands Conflict that resonates with me most. Under repeated air attack he observes that "yet again training and delegation saved us". This remains as true now, as it did then. This is why the Royal Navy in the 21st Century continues to place a premium on high quality training to produce highly capable and versatile people. It is also why we continue to impress upon our sailors and marines, and those who lead them, the importance of delegation – by employing something of that Nelsonian 'mission command'. That ability to give clear intent, and then *trust* your people to decide how best to deliver that intent.

Perhaps above all, it is in this book that we deepen our appreciation of why the art of leadership, no more so than at sea, continues to endure.

Mark Stanhope

INTRODUCTION

Dare we imagine that we have caused more than a ripple in this world? In my personal span of 77 years from 1935 to the present day I have witnessed and experienced many social changes, career challenges and fantastic opportunities. I have briefed Mrs Thatcher. I have been fired at by Exocet missiles. I have water skied behind a minesweeper and swum with the sharks. I have lined the route at the Queen's Coronation, danced in a tutu and attended Royal Princesses. I have also been mugged in Jamaica, and had an ape named after me in Gibraltar. I have marvelled at new technology and given grateful thanks to old and well made engines.

In this book I have tried to give both glimpses of my life experiences and more considered depth to the more serious moments of my career in the Royal Navy. It is nearly 30 years since the most challenging time in the Falklands conflict. By covering my personal journey I hope that it will help society recognise the value of the highly trained personnel and ships that make up the modern navy, and illustrate why it is such a great institution in times of war and peace – as both a deterrent, a reassurance and as an ambassador.

The sea has always captured my imagination. Many writers have written about its mysterious attraction. Very few writers have attempted to analyse its special qualities and how these qualities might affect modern, military operations. No one would dispute that maritime operations are sufficiently different to warrant a specialised approach and a different understanding.

The battle might be won or lost, enterprises might succeed or miscarry, territories might be gained or quitted, but what dominates our ability to carry on in a war, is the mastery of the ocean routes and the free approach and entry to our ports.

Everyone in the world has had experience of operating on the land while only a small percentage of the world population has been to sea. This means that most people, policy makers and strategists are unfamiliar with the environment and the special nature of operations and what that means to policy strategy and tactics. States conduct war on the land, in order to achieve long term political control over a territory. Warfare at sea, on the other hand, is concerned with the temporary control over commerce or denial of use to an adversary of sea areas, with the purpose of influencing what is taking place on the land. Maritime operations involve the transport and delivery of the world's commerce, using it for political and economic purposes in peacetime and in the conducting of war. History demonstrates that man has sought control of the sea areas in a very different manner and for very different reasons and purposes than he has sought control over the land.

Despite the fact that large ocean areas have recently become subject to limited state sovereignty, the natural state of the seas is one of absence of control, whereas the natural state of the land will remain one of control by sovereign powers.

Forces at sea might be out of sight and out of mind. But in peacetime, crisis or war this force might be decisive. Naval forces can be sent to the scene at smaller political cost than any other military force. Additionally, naval forces arrive ready to carry out the tasks they might be assigned. They need no major logistic support from overseas bases, nor do they require access to overflying rights and they have staying power, inherent mobility and flexibility making them an ideal instrument to blend varying foreign office policies. They can be withdrawn easily when the job is done, leaving behind no strong physical reminders but strong symbolic ones. States routinely use their navies to make political statements well beyond their immediate borders.

Rear Admiral Joseph Caldwell Wylie, the much respected American Naval Strategist when quoted in an article on *The Royal Navy in the 21st Century* by Eric J Grove (author of *The Royal Navy Since 1815*) in the Centenary Issue of the Mariners Mirror 2011 – described the navy thus:

This almost indefinable quality of maritime presence – subtle, benign, ubiquitous presence – actual or potential presence – is a great asset of sea power in times of peace even in times of one or another variety of tension. This quality of actual or even potential maritime presence anywhere round the world is the quality that sets navies apart from armies and air forces as employment short of war. This worldwide and benign ubiquity the subtle evidence of navy and thus national strength is what makes viable other normally benign elements of national strength when extended overseas.

The spirit of the navy is too old, varied and too subtle to be adequately interpreted by any outsider no matter how keen their interest or affection. In peace the navy exists under conditions that may take years of training to understand, and the modern naval personnel are subject to a set of physical and mental strains that are very different from the bloodier and primitive times of the Battle of Trafalgar.

These modern men and women need to be trained and led in every generation, for at the end of the day it is the people that make the ultimate sacrifice not the machinery. We can believe and thank God that, judging from our thousand year old past, no body of men, from within or without, can kill the spirit of the navy.

During my life I have enjoyed the firm handrail of my faith without which I could not have achieved so much.

I hope this book shows the value of the courage I have witnessed and which I have had the honour to experience in my naval career. I have always been humbled by the display of humanity at its finest and leadership at its best.

PART 1

THE START OF SOMETHING BIG

Chapter 1

FIRST SEA LEGS

My first sea adventure was at the age of 14 as a member of the sea scouts. Our Shoreham-by-sea-based troop went on a long weekend to London, spending the nights moored alongside Waterloo Bridge on *HMS Discovery*, which was the explorer Captain Scott's ship.

Our stay coincided with the Oxford and Cambridge Universities boat race which is rowed annually on the River Thames from Putney to Mortlake. Inspired by this event the troop leaders loaded us into a small cutter and exhorted us to row the whole course. We were eight oars, and although we didn't row in competition or at the same time as the famous race, we rowed all those 4 miles 374 yards in rather more than the record breaking 16 minutes 19 seconds but we felt like winners anyway.

So my sea going adventures had started off well but I was unsure whether I wanted to make the Royal Navy my career, which was what my father wished. My father was born and educated in South Africa. His father, an academic and linguist was one of the founders of Rhodes University in Grahamstown SA.

He was only ten years old when his younger brother Valentin died of an extreme form of pneumonia. He determined from that moment to study medicine, as he felt very strongly that his brother could have been saved with the right treatment. In the early 20th century there were no wonder drugs like penicillin, which was not commercially produced until the 1940s, and infections like pneumonia or septicemia were killer diseases.

He chose to study at Guys Hospital in London, intending to specialise in Paediatrics. Unfortunately, he too suffered from a severe bout of pneumonia and returned to South Africa to convalesce for two years.

On his return, friends persuaded him to forgo training as a Specialist which would take at least another expensive three or four years and instead aim to become a General Practitioner. One of the reasons for this choice was that students had to pay for their tuition bed and board, and as medical training is lengthy, lack of funds and mounting debts loomed large. He had no private income to fall back on, a problem young medical students are facing again today.

To start work as a GP you had to either buy into a practice or put your brass plate up and hope patients would find their way to you. To buy into an established practice was expensive, medical expertise and natural charm were not enough. The social hoops you had to jump through to be accepted were incomprehensible to a young man from South Africa who had not experienced these particular social mores and who did not have the funds to buy his way in.

While working at Brighton Hospital, he met a charming wealthy old lady, who impressed by his medical skill and his bedside manner, suggested he came to the small village where she lived to join the established practice there and she offered to sponsor him. The other doctors at the existing practice had different ideas and felt my father was unsuitable. So in September 1934 my father rented a flat in the centre of town and put his brass plate up on the front door.

He persuaded my mother, a nurse he had met at Brighton Hospital, to join him, and they lived and worked happily together in Steyning, West Sussex for the rest of their lives.

In 1939, my father decided to support his adopted country by joining the Royal Navy, in which he served as a doctor until the end of the war. His love of the RN never dimmed and he was a keen member of the Royal Naval Volunteer Reserve (RNVR)[1] until he retired in his eighties, by then having been promoted to an Honorary Surgeon Captain.

He realised that the RN offered young men wide ranging opportunities, to travel and experience a diverse lifestyle, an impossible dream for most young people in that gloomy post war era.

That was why he encouraged me to look at a career in the RN, and with certain misgivings I decided to take the Civil Service Commission exams, which at that time you had to pass to gain a place at the Royal Naval College Dartmouth[2]. It was normal to take them after your first year of A level study. I took these exams in London and, before I knew it, I was on my way to the Admiralty for interviews.

In the 1950s the Royal Navy was extraordinarily keen on good eyesight. It wasn't necessary to have 20/20 vision, but they were very wary of any defects, for good reason. At that time, the bridges of ships were open, there was no protection from weather, waves or wind and a constant spray bathed your eyes. Those wearing glasses would either lose them or they would repeatedly mist up. Any other weakness would be exacerbated by the constant onslaught on your exposed eyes by the weather conditions, so the Admiralty and the RN took any eye weaknesses very seriously.

We had been summoned to a large building in the MoD in London for our Royal Naval College medical. We would receive a medical check in London and then proceed to Dartmouth by train, for further aptitude tests at the college.

To ascertain whether we suffered from any eye problems, candidates for interview had special drops put into their eyes, then after approximately one hour the medical staff checked for any lurking or undiscovered optical disease. These drops caused blurred vision, which we were assured would pass leaving us bright eyed and bushy tailed by the time we reached The Naval College, a five hour train journey from London.

The medical examination over, eight of us were lined up behind a member of the college staff and instructed to put our hand on the shoulder of the cadet in front. So, in one long bleary-eyed crocodile formation, the future hierarchy of the RN, weaved their way blindly across London to the train station.

The need for the Officer of the Watch to have A1 eyesight receded with the advent of the enclosed bridge in 1966 a very welcome and infinitely more comfortable development.

The interviews the next day were in two sittings. The first concerned engineering ability and was followed by a rather frightening mass interrogation by a group of senior officers chaired by an Admiral.

The first interview went rather well, but I felt very nervous as I opened the door to the interview room for my second. My father's advice was ringing in my ears: 'Look ahead and walk forward purposefully and with confidence.' Unfortunately, his advice missed out the contingency of a large dog owned by the Admiral stretched across my path. As I tripped over this dog causing it to yelp, I experienced the same sensation as that of a young man standing on the deck of a sinking ship. As I looked up I noticed the assembled board was hiding a serious fit of giggles behind their hands. Despite my accident I was still offered a place.

Three months later the successful candidates for RN officer training all boarded the train to Dartmouth, wearing our ill-fitting uniforms from Gieves, the famous tailor. These had been sent to each of us at home and, looking at the motley crew on the train, I would guess that the measurements for these uniforms were in the *one size fits all* category. They were definitely not up to their renowned bespoke quality.

On arrival at Kingswear station, we boarded a ferry to cross the River Dart.

Disembarking tired after our journey and a little apprehensive, we formed up, kitbags on our shoulders, ready to march up the rather long steep hill to the college.

One of our number, an ex-maritime school alumnae, was very keen from the word go to show our instructors that he meant business. As few of us had ever marched in our lives, he took it upon himself, as a marching expert to keep us in line. He illustrated his ambition by yelling at us to keep pace all the way up the hill. By the time we reached the college, we were in a muck sweat, with dark murder in our hearts.

On our first day at Dartmouth College we were all told to stand around the perimeters of the parade ground. No one told us why we should be doing this, but we realised that as the most junior officers in the RN, you did as you were told.

The Chief Petty Officer came down to see us and, wandering round the cadets, he pointed to us apparently at random saying: 'You, you and you.'

We all hoped he was picking us out as future First Sea Lords. In fact, he was selecting those who were about the same height, a disappointment at first but this feeling was soon replaced with genuine excitement. By dint of our height, we were chosen to form part of the street lining guard for Queen Elizabeth II's Coronation Day in London.

This memorable duty involved learning to stand still for hours at an end, doing without food and water for as many hours, and learning not to faint (if you must faint, faint backwards). It was worth every excruciating minute.

The chosen cadets from Sandhurst (Army), Cranwell (Royal Air Force) and Dartmouth (RN) were taken by bus to Sandhurst. At 3.40am on Coronation day we travelled to London by train. On arrival we marched to our given places. Our group was lined up right across Whitehall when she passed as Princess Elizabeth, and right across Westminster Bridge when she passed as Her Majesty the Queen.

It was an exciting, thrilling, wonderful sight and the crowd was warm and magnificent. We stood in line for hours with our hands behind our backs, and the amiable crowd kept putting sweets in them, which we ate surreptitiously. They really kept us going.

One of the most gratifying outcomes of the day was the effect of the continuous rain on my ill-fitting Gieves suit. The soaking had caused it to shrink to size and become a perfect fit.

My father also celebrated my starring role by buying our first 10 inch black and white television, so that our family and many friends could relish every moment of the Queen's Coronation. The new media, television, offered the UK and the Empire's population unprecedented access to a Royal occasion.

At the end of our term at Dartmouth, the final address was given by the Captain of the college. It started as follows:

You are the worst term in the entire history of the college. You have reduced the discipline of the gunroom to zero.

Being part of that notorious group was probably not the best start to my naval career.

Notes

1. The Royal Naval Volunteer Reserve (RNVR) was formed in 1903 and ceased to exist in 1958. Many of the volunteer officers transferred to the newly formed Royal Naval Reserve (RNR).

2. The Royal Naval College Dartmouth is now known as Britannia Royal Naval College and has been training officers in Dartmouth, Devon since 1905. The mission statement for the college reads: '*To deliver courageous leaders with the spirit to fight and win.*'

Chapter 2

HMS TRIUMPH

After three months at Dartmouth, now 18 years old, we were all appointed to the aircraft carrier *HMS Triumph*[1], then used as the cadet training ship, for 2 terms. In the spring she travelled to the West Indies, in summer to the Baltic and in autumn the Mediterranean.

The idea was for the young cadets to see all stages and grades of operation and get the feel of what the Royal Navy did at sea and learn how to behave in foreign countries.

To be honest, at that time in history it was like a government run finishing school for young men. After the gloom and doom of the Second World War, the 1950s navy offered a golden opportunity to travel to far-flung places and experience the sheer wonders of the world, allowing us to meet a huge range of people, eat unheard of foods and gain some spit and polish.

Triumph *in the West Indies.*

Despite these opportunities the young cadet was way down the pecking order and did not rate much respect from either officers or crew. As cadets we were allocated to a part of the ship under the aegis of a Petty Officer and were responsible for the cleanliness of that part of the ship.

At 6.30 every morning, the cadets lined up with a scrubber in one hand, trousers rolled up and bare feet. The duty Petty Officer in charge turned on the cold water hoses and we were set out to scrub our bit of deck clean. Once the scrubbing met the Petty Officer's approval we moved on to polishing the brass. If this was done acceptably it took about ten minutes. Luckily for me my cleaning area led off the forecastle at the bulkhead. This stroke of luck placed me at our final mustering point and more importantly right by the doorway leading to the most important event of the day – breakfast. I led the charge down to breakfast each morning ensuring a hearty meal. If you dawdled or were at the back of the queue your time was at best severely curtailed and at worst you missed the meal altogether and had to wait until lunch for food.

My journey as a cadet in the RN was a wonderful learning curve. Being whisked off on a large aircraft carrier, at the age of 18 to the sparkling seas of the West Indies was a dream come true for a young man used to the grey drabness of post war Britain. Cadets may have been considered lower down the career ladder than anyone, but you can put up with a lot if you are looking at a Caribbean sky.

At one time in college, I had been studying the curved bow of an aircraft carrier and mused on how it could possibly be painted. Well, in the West Indies I discovered the methodology.

Step one involves rigging up a whole series of nets. At first they hang vertically like curtains hanging off the decks. Step two involves pulling the nets tight and fastening to a set of cleats which are already in situ. These in turn form net bags through which you cling and clamber.

At the end of the procedure you have the bow covered in netting and the netting filled with hundreds of drone-like cadets, carrying paintbrushes and paint pots filled with Admiralty grey paint. The cadets descended daily down this extraordinary structure and painted as long as they could.

You first grabbed one of the ropes and hauled yourself in, scrambling along the nets and continuing to paint moving in and out as you travelled along the ship's side. All was well. Morale was high, our bodies were turning nut brown and we had the Caribbean at our feet.

There was lots of sunshine to bask in and crystal clear water to swim in. Then a minor occurrence took place. Someone dropped a scrubbing brush from the netting where it fell in the water with a loud splash. Suddenly there was a huge swirl in the water and a shark came up and grabbed the brush. Suddenly the water looked less

Triumph *alongside Gibraltar.*

Gibraltar.

inviting. We were in a state of perpetual fright, we could not get off the netting fast enough. Our Caribbean dream had become a thing of nightmares. The duty officer who had the tiresome job of looking after us and was unimpressed with our fears said, with steel in his voice, 'I shall go out in a boat and check the paintwork. I shall then tell you what needs to be done.'

He came back and told us we had missed a large area of paintwork mainly due to the fact that we had spent more time shark spotting than checking the side of the ship. There was genuine fear coursing through our veins as, with much trepidation, we went out to finish the job. Beauty truly is only surface deep.

We were still serving on *HMS Triumph,* heading towards the Mediterranean from our magical sojourn in the West Indies, when we were suddenly instructed to change course and head full steam towards Algiers. A troop ship, the *Empire Windrush,* carrying both troops and their families was on fire opposite the Port of Algiers.

Washing up.

Some of the survivors.

The ship was ablaze from end to end, flames shooting vertically into the sky. It was amazing that only four people died, considering how many wives and children were on board. It could have been a much greater tragedy.

The survivors were taken into Algiers, where we were to pick them up and take them on to Gibraltar, where Lady Mountbatten was waiting to receive them.

We did not take long to get to Gibraltar, but on the way we young cadets were given one of the most unusual duties I ever had in the RN. Each of us was posted outside various cabins and rooms to act as bottle babies. A single disembodied arm would stretch out from the cabin and the hand would be clasping an empty bottle. This was a sign for the cadet to leap down the gangway and take the bottle to the chef. The chef filled the bottle with warm milk and the cadet then took it back to the mother concerned.

It was my first experience of the social role played by the armed forces who are trained not only to fight, but also to work as a protective force too.

At the end of our last term on the training ship, *HMS Triumph*, I was apparently level pegging with another candidate for the prize of the Sword of Honour, given to the best cadet of the year. To decide who deserved it, they gave both of us the same task. I lost – but the best man won. My brother salvaged the family pride by winning the Sword of Honour a few years later.

Notes
1. *HMS Triumph*, Light Fleet Aircraft Carrier – Colossus Class. Built by Hawthorn Leslie and Company on the Tyne. She was launched in 1944. She served in the Korean War and was used for the first trials of the angled flight deck in 1952. In 1954 she became the cadet training ship but her role was scrapped when the training schedule changed. She was converted to a heavy repair and transport ship and was based in Singapore. Put into reserve in 1975 she was used as a feature on navy open days in Chatham dockyard. She was scrapped in 1981.

Chapter 3

HMS VANGUARD

HMS Vanguard[1] was built to be the biggest, fastest Royal Navy battleship. In spite of this she never fired her guns in anger, as she was not commissioned until after the war in 1946.

Her big moment came in 1947, when she took the whole Royal Family on a state visit to South Africa. This trip marked the first time Princess Elizabeth had travelled abroad and gave the Royal Family the chance to recuperate from the stresses and strain of the war. George VI had also been very ill and the sea voyage was a perfect and private convalescence.

A huge additional infrastructure, called The King's Quarters, had been added to the deck area, to act as appropriate accommodation for a reigning monarch. For some unknown reason this royal space was built right in the line of sight for the after guns on board. Firing of these guns was absolutely verboten as the Royal Family would have been blown to smithereens.

With the commission of a new royal yacht, *HMRY Britannia* in 1954, *HMS Vanguard* took a step down the social ladder and became a training ship for young midshipmen, my lowly status at that time.

I joined *Vanguard* in May 1954. She was the Flag Ship for the Home Fleet, so I was one of the privileged crews who steamed past the Queen as she returned home from a six-month absence visiting her Empire in her new Royal Yacht.

In fact, Her Majesty had made most of her journey round the Empire in the SS *Gothic* steamship, only picking up her new yacht on the way home in Tobruk, Libya.

A part of the Royal Navy's remit is to act as guardian to Her Majesty when she is on board her Royal Yacht. In those days the RN was split between the Home Fleet ships that policed home waters, and the Mediterranean Fleet, ships that protected the seas of the British Empire. As *HMRY Britannia* steamed towards home waters from Gibraltar she reverted from the protection of the Med Fleet to the guardianship of the Home Fleet.

This Royal Homecoming review was going to be a very impressive and unique line-up with the two fleets steaming past *HMRY Britannia*. At 3pm all hands fell in on the ship and we were manned and ready. In addition to ourselves there were submarines of all classes and a good number of destroyers and frigates.

Vanguard *passing Royal Yacht.*

At 5pm the whole fleet started to steam past. The two lines of escort ships fenced in the royal yacht and from this position every ship turned inwards until they were just 200 yards from an imaginary protective line drawn in the sea. They then turned parallel to the yacht and commenced the steam past.

As soon as the rear of this first column had passed us, *HMS Apollo* drew astern of us and overtook on our starboard side. We then followed in her wake.

Vanguard *firing her 15" guns.*

As we drew abreast we gave three cheers for Her Majesty the Queen. The Royal Family was standing just aft of a glass viewing box as the Home Fleet turned away. Four fast patrol boats flying the flag of Commander in Chief Portsmouth took over the escort through the Needles and along the South Coast. At 18.30 we stopped and transferred the press who had been on board *Vanguard* to record the scene.

The Queen sent us a signal thanking us for the escort and the order came through to splice the main brace.[2]

The thousands of loyal subjects lined up along the south coast missed most of this display as bad weather and sea fog persisted. The small boat enthusiasts showed their Dunkirk spirit by braving the adverse conditions and heading for rather suicidal positions amongst the serried columns of RN vessels.

This could have turned a wonderful occasion into a disaster as a battleship bearing down on a small yacht in the fog leaves little room for escape. The Signals Officer on board the flag ship did an absolutely sterling job ensuring their safety by flailing arms and flags in true Reggie Perrin manner.

* * * * *

The Royal Yacht.

Passing the Royal Yacht, ready to salute the Queen.

The Queen (circled).

Left: King Gustav Arriving. Right: Inspecting the Royal Marines.

HMS Vanguard may have been a little outdated by naval standards, but she was a magnificent battleship and my three months on board offered endlessly exhilarating experiences.

On one trip we were anchored in the Strait of Oresund which runs between Sweden and Denmark, Helsinger and Helsingor respectively. I and another midshipman were on boat running duties. This unenviable 24-hour task involved running 150 Liberty men[3] ashore in two 45ft launches just after we anchored, then returning them to the ship throughout the night until the following morning.

A large group of sailors liberally oiled with Skol can be a little troublesome.

On our return journey, if a loud cheer emitted from the group as we berthed alongside, the Officer of the Watch would invariably send us round the ship for a second sobering circuit. A large dose of sea spray and a rain shower would usually have the desired calming effect. If not, we went round and round the ship until a drenched silence descended on the human cargo.

On the following morning, my fellow driver and I had just handed over our boats and descended to the gun room for lunch when we received a message from on high.

We were to report to the quarter deck at 3pm and go ashore in the Commander in Chief's barge. This was very special and painted a wonderful racing green, colloquially known as the green parrot.

We were instructed to collect some rather select guests: the Royal Princesses.

We had heard that the Swedish Royal Family had been playing host to the Danish Royal Family. We also knew that the Swedish Princesses were 17 and 18 years old. We were 19 years old, and thrilled at the prospect of hosting two royal stunners.

At the harbour, the crowds lined the quay waiting to see the Royal Princesses arrive. A large black car pulled up and out got the Danish Royal Princesses, 12, seven and five years old respectively. A momentary look of regret passed across our faces but they were in fact lovely, inquisitive and lively. We showed them round the large battleship and gave them tea in the King's Quarters, where their British counterparts had stayed on their state trip to South Africa. One of the princesses is now Queen Margrethe of Denmark.

Arriving on board.

King Gustav VI Adolf of Sweden, inspecting the top division.

Regatta.

*   *   *   *   *

It is very important to keep a ship's company fit. There are not that many sports you can do at sea but occasionally the Home Fleet would anchor and put on a regatta.

It was all very exciting and every ship would enter as many boats as it could.

These varied from sailing boats to the very heavy whalers, clinker – built with even heavier oars, which *HMS Vanguard* entered.

Regatta Supporters.

Regatta Finishing Post.

Five sailors rowed and the sixth acted as a sort of cox. It was not quite on a par with the famous Oxford and Cambridge boat race but the enthusiasm and competition between the individual crews was right up there!

We would set down in the sea and practise at 6.30 every morning until the day of the big race. The whalers were the last race of the day. We set off with a whoosh of spray and a determined spirit. We won.

Midshipmen were encouraged to be adventurous and to think outside of the box. Team work was essential and problem solving paramount. So piratical raids on other ships, while not officially encouraged, were part of the midshipman's and ordinary sailor's traditional training.

A raid would be carried out just before dawn and the normal booty would be something like a lifebelt or jacket. It would be returned in the morning, after a formal request had been made from the raided party. Our classic raid involved both the midshipmen (Gunroom) and the sailors (boys). The Gunroom came down in

Home Fleet Regatta Race Course.

one launch on the port side of the target frigate and the boys in a launch on the starboard side. With split second timing both groups swamped the upper deck of the ship and we stripped her of everything including the logbooks. Within minutes both launches sped off loaded with our spoils.

Much to our amazement no one seemed to be aware of our raid, and a rather shamefaced Captain of the raided frigate had to call the Commander in Chief the following morning to find out who had raided the ship and to ensure the return of all the objects we had removed.

After three months we left *HMS Vanguard*. This battleship should have been one of the stars of the Home Fleet. In fact her starring roles were as a temporary Royal Yacht and as a stand in for a ship in the film *Sink the Bismark*. Her problem which became apparent during early trials, was a fault in the design. This made the stresses on her hull to be in excess for those expected on a new ship. It was decided therefore that *Vanguard* should never put to sea if the displacement exceeded the design figure of 49,200 tons except in a time of real emergency. To ensure absolute safety she was restricted to a speed of 20 knots, way below an acceptable speed for a ship of her calibre.

Notes

1. HMS VANGUARD was the last battleship to be built for the RN and the last built in the world. She was built by John Brown and company Clydebank Scotland. Not finished until the end of World War Two she had varied roles ending her career as the flagship of the Royal Navy Reserve Force. She played a starring role in the film *Sink the Bismark*. Sold for scrap 1960.

2. Splice the Mainbrace has nothing to do with sails. Her Majesty the Queen can order STM in recognition of outstanding support from her fleet such as this homecoming. It means that every man and woman in the fleet receives an extra tot of rum which is an eighth of a pint. The daily tot of rum has been replaced by beer as those imbibing were not as alert as they should be after partaking of the tot. Each ship has to have a supply of rum on board in case the reigning monarch orders Splice the Mainbrace. The origin of the phrase comes from the act of splicing a new rope into the main stays, a very difficult and dangerous job.

3. Liberty men is the name given to sailors allowed ashore for time off, literally meaning liberty.

Chapter 4

HMS SUPERB AND
APPOINTMENT TO SUB LIEUTENANT

HMS Superb[1] was my last posting as a young midshipman. She had a fairly unremarkable career in RN terms but I will always have a deep affection for her and the part she played in my continuing education. For a young man in the 1950s joining the Navy had been a wondrous step in opening up vistas and opportunities only attainable, up to that point, to the very, very, very rich.

In less than a year, I and the rest of the ship's company travelled 37,000 miles around the World. We visited countries that were just distant names on a map to the average young person. We experienced lifestyles which, before this trip, had only been synonymous with the glamour of the Hollywood movie. We met beautiful and influential people and were plied with the kind of food and drink we had only been able to imagine during the war and the ration-smitten years following it.

Superb.

The British Empire was rapidly diminishing, but the RN still flew the flag around the world, training young officers and sailors to the highest standards.

The quarters and collective term for young, naval officers and midshipmen on a ship is 'the Gunroom'. The Gunroom of *HMS Superb* was a feisty crowd with strong magpie tendencies. Our particular penchant was for signage. No interesting sign escaped our purloining fingers and, as we travelled the globe, the Gunroom filled with 'borrowed' miscellanea.

At the start of our great voyage we were 'working up' the ship in Portland. This involved storing up the ship for the voyage, trialing and testing the engines and all the mechanisms and checking the crew understood their roles and the correct procedures for every possible contingency on the ship. While this was taking place we would normally be berthed alongside at night so the ship's company was allowed shore leave. Three members of our Gunroom decided that what we needed was a physical reminder of our green and pleasant land as we travelled the globe. With this end in mind, under the cloak of darkness, they went ashore with screwdrivers and started to remove the Lloyds Bank sign in Weymouth High Street. Unfortunately, a member of the constabulary, who was standing unnoticed in a shop doorway, witnessed this act of patriotic vandalism and arrested all three. They appeared in court the following morning and were fined £3 each, a large dent in a midshipman's salary in those days.

A larger blot on their copybooks was the fact that the new Commodore had just taken over command of the ship and had intended to sail on the dot of 8am. As a result of their overnight detention, the sailing was postponed until 10.30am, when the three chastened midshipmen slunk up the gangplank – poorer but wiser.

We set sail from Portland and after about eight days of pretty rough weather we woke up to find the temperature had risen and the skies were blue. We were in Bermuda and learnt the joys of swimming in October. Having cleared the water of sharks with 1lb scarers of dynamite, we began slowly exchanging our pale washed-out pallor for deep Bermudian tans.

The Captain invited our first guests on board for a cocktail party, a new form of entertainment in most of our lives and one the ship was expected to offer the local dignitaries and prominent ex pats, at every port of call. We also encountered for the first time the serious danger of an over-indulgence of any cocktail mix.

After ten days of acclimatising we headed towards the now infamous Guantanamo Bay, Cuba, a three-day sail from Bermuda. We were to exercise with the US Navy. On arrival we used the usual method of clearing the sea of sharks, and jumped into the Caribbean.

Guantanamo Bay was even then a US base. It afforded a huge range of the usual sporting facilities and recreational pursuits, up to the more unusual big game fishing, horse riding and even ice skating. I had always avoided horse riding, horses rather scare me, but as the Gunroom was invited I felt obliged to go. I managed to stay on the horse, which perhaps gave me a false sense of self confidence in my mastery of the breed. I would pay for it later.

There was Coca Cola on tap and the more impressively – to the ration-starved Brits – the PX/NEX stores (department stores based on US military bases and selling a huge range of consumer goods) that were like an Aladdin's cave to us. As if these luxuries were not enough, we also experienced the famous American Snack Shack offering hamburgers, t-bone steaks and ribs. This menu was sheer, unadulterated, greedy luxury for us.

These perks might make our stay sound like one long holiday, but during our two-week sojourn we were mainly at sea, on very testing Exercise with our American allies, so a bit of relaxation and fun was needed.

After the first week of acknowledging that the American Fleet had far superior equipment than us and the joint exercises illustrating just how ancient a lot of our equipment was in comparison to theirs, it was great to be able to show off, with the aid of the unique Royal Marine Band.

We staged our Military Tattoo with the Royal Marine Band starring, as only they can, on the airstrip under huge arc lights and in front of an audience of thousands. Tattoos are impressive, and the British are very good at them, and this performance was no exception. So with American cheers ringing in our ears, we set off for Haiti.

In Port au Prince, the capital of Haiti, we were to pick up President Tubman of Liberia, who had been on a goodwill visit to the hurricane-ravaged city. We were then to take him onwards to Jamaica. I have no idea why. We anchored about 2 miles offshore and gave the 21-gun salute, the military way of welcoming an honoured guest.

This was meant to be a quick pick up, but the President ran late with his programme. As a consequence, he was not piped aboard until 19.00. More surprisingly for the catering staff, he was accompanied by an entourage of 15 people. In typical naval fashion no one was fazed and he sat down to a superb dinner with the Commodore.

It was the hurricane season and as were running several hours late we had to press on to Jamaica at 25 knots. A rough sea traversed at high speed does not bode well for a good night's sleep. I think President Tubman was very pleased to arrive in Jamaica and get back on to dry land. We all were.

*　*　*　*　*

I will always remember Jamaica for two main reasons. First because I was mugged and second because I confirmed my fear of horses, vowing never to ride one again.

Kingston was cheap and the entertainment in the town offered rum, women and calypso. Unfortunately, if you wandered off the main street, which I and two friends did, you encountered a darker side to the city. After a trip to the cinema, the three of us took a short cut and ended up in a dark alleyway between two main streets. We were halfway down when a group of men came out of the shadows. We were held up at knifepoint while they ripped off our watches. We swung at them, got rabbit punches in return, and then they ran off melting away into the shadows.

In a police station later we were told there were up to 60 gangsters working the area. They produced a book of mug shots featuring the main gentlemen of the island with a penchant for robbery. We ploughed our way through books of photos trying to identify our attackers, but we were unsuccessful and we went back to the ship disconsolate.

On our return, the Gunroom exploded with anger. It was decided that the whole Gunroom would go ashore the next night, find the perpetrators and sort them out. So, armed with a variety of offensive weapons, baseball bats and golf clubs, we stalked the streets. Fortunately, with hindsight, these particular gentlemen of the road had the good sense to keep out of sight and we returned to the ship, feeling honour was satisfied.

At one of the many cocktail parties we were invited to, in Jamaica, I met a charming plantation owner. His crop was sugar cane and he invited a few of us to lunch.

After a superb meal, he suggested that we might like to ride through the plantation on horseback. My friends demurred but I, fool that I am, leapt at the chance.

Headed for a fall.

We walked down to a small barn where a pure white horse (apparently, called a grey) waited tied to a tree.

A young Jamaican was also standing there with a bicycle. He was to escort me round the area and point out the route. I mounted the horse and immediately felt a strong sense of foreboding.

My guide and I walked through the rows of sugar cane and I began to relax. My confidence increased when my companion said, 'Sir is a mighty fine rider!' a huge grin crossing his face. Reaching the river we stopped for the horse to drink and then turned for home. Anyone who has ridden a horse knows that they tend to go faster on the return journey back to their field or stable. This horse was no exception. In fact, before we had completed the turn homewards, he was off, in a flat out gallop, neck stretched out, ears flattened, with his rider hanging on for dear life. My bicycling companion, left in our wake, stood watching our retreating forms. As the barn came into view and the horse knew he was on the way home, he slowed to a canter, then a walk. My eyes were raised heavenward in silent prayer. As I slid out of the saddle and my feet touched dry land, I felt my legs turn to water, so I held on to the saddle. At that moment my guide came pedalling furiously into the yard, with a look of huge relief on his face when he saw me in one piece.

My friends, meanwhile, were enjoying a rum punch on the veranda, which had given them a perfect view of my speedy return. The smirks were only half hidden. I vowed never to mount a horse again.

Montego Bay was very different from Kingston. Wonderful, palm-fringed beaches with pure white sands and crystal clear warm water. Beach barbeques were the norm and the chance to see flying fish leap and dolphins play lured us into buying snorkelling equipment so we could experience the sights under the water too.

Even more glamour was added by the arrival of a group of Christian Dior models, who had been putting on catwalk shows in Kingston and were now doing the same in Montego Bay. These beautiful willowy girls adorned the beach and the cocktail parties.

There was a slight hiccough to all this hedonism and it came in the form of sea anemones. Their favourite spot was where the sea met the sand, so when running in or out of the water or along the beach you could tread on them very easily; this meant you went from athletic sprint to hobble in seconds, and the spikes were difficult to remove safely. Wounded by one of these I hobbled up the beach, to be approached by one of the Dior models. Leading me by the hand she magically produced a bowl of hot wax which, when put on the wound, drew out the spike. I fell in love immediately but her Florence Nightingale moment over, she wafted away to her friends, never to be seen again by me.

*　*　*　*　*

We returned to our home base in Bermuda to get ready for Christmas celebrations, both on and off the ship. Our arrival coincided with the arrival of a squadron of four ships from the Canadian Navy. We had a great time together but they had to leave after a few days.

A very strong wind was blowing making it hard for ships to get off the jetty. One of their destroyers, in what proved an unwise move, backed off and started to swing very dangerously. Their instinct was to go full ahead, to stop the swinging. Unfortunately, by doing this they did not make the harbour entrance, but instead hit smack into the harbour wall.

Already in serious trouble, they were rather incredibly told by their senior officer to drop anchor immediately. They followed this order and let go the anchor. This had been holding up the bow, the bow dropped 45 degrees, and they collided with the other wall. This was a lesson burnt into my brain, and it stayed with me as a terrible warning whenever backing off a jetty.

Back in the base we had, as is the practice, put together a review show called *We Ain't Sulkin'* as an entertainment for the ship's company and our hosts. After some of the Bermudians saw the show at our base, we were invited to put it on at the Bermudian Theatre, where we played to a packed house and raised a good sum for charity.

My performance with two others involved three net tutus, some balletic gyrations with three balloons and quite a considerable amount of rubbing our bodies together. This all played out to strains from the ballet *Coppelia* which I can never hear without thinking of that time. There were many uplifting moments, including a grand performance by the ship's choir who belted out a collection of songs and carols so well that they were broadcast on local radio.

For the next couple of weeks we took on stores for our long voyage to South America. We had had a great Christmas but it was time to get back out to sea.

A few days into January we anchored off Nassau. The sea had a big swell, but you can't stop a ship's company from exploring new territory. So about 200 of us went ashore by liberty boat and had a swim or went to the market. The wind began to rise and it was soon obvious we were marooned ashore for the night. It was then the people of Nassau showed their generosity. We were literally scooped up and taken to parties, dinners and luxurious mansions. Those left on the ship had a rotten time in the storm and, eventually, had to weigh anchor and move to a more sheltered position.

The next morning we made it back to the ship, which repaid the islanders kindness by hosting a party on board. Part of our job was to fly the flag and promote good-will by entertaining the local population, as well as the great and the good at the places we visited. Getting everything shipshape for this impromptu celebration gave us a dummy run for the many children's parties and cocktail parties the ship would host on the rest of the tour.

We sailed off to Jamaica for refuelling and after a brief stay finally sailed towards the great Panama Canal. Ready and waiting to go in, we were approached by a medical officer who insisted the whole ship was sprayed with DDT before we went through. So, with our Commodore in charge, a man who got things done, the whole ship was fumigated in less than an hour and we were on our way through the canal. Only those essential to safety stayed below deck. The rest of the ship's company was on deck to experience the sheer glory of this engineering feat. We were being towed from one lock to another watching, as the pilots towed us through, the ever changing jungles and lakes. Some seemed frighteningly narrow and we wondered whether we would collide with the ships coming the other way. But these pilots really knew their stuff and within ten hours we were in the Pacific Ocean. And I saw my first alligator.

For the next few days we steamed south to the Equator and late one night a motley crowd of sea creatures came aboard and addressed the Commodore. This group demanded we stop and ready ourselves to meet King Neptune. This big fat Neptune laid down the rules for the ceremony of *Crossing The Line* the next day, then disappeared back over the side.

The equator runs through the centre of the Earth and crossing this imaginary line is traditionally celebrated by fun and festivities overseen by King Neptune and his courtiers. These are, of course, the ship's company dressed as such.

The next day, his royal presence duly arrived with his Queen, clerks and sea nymphs. Warrants were read out, but only distinguished members of the crew avoided punishment. The rest of us were treated to the complete ablutions, dunked under water, draped with seaweed and painted as sea creatures. Those trying to escape were sought out and dragged to their punishment. It was my first, best and unforgettable *Crossing the Line*.

In a matter of days we arrived in Callao, the main seaport for Lima the capital of Peru. We were inundated with invitations. As a visiting foreign naval ship, both the British ex pats and the Peruvians gave us a wonderful time.

The Lima Cricket Club insisted all bar tabs were on the house. The so-called Peruvian cricket team seemed to be made up of mainly ex pats.

We gave our first Children's Party, an entertainment which we repeated over and over again for the local children in the towns and cities we visited. When we transformed our ship into a piratical fantasy world, we were uncertain how it would all work, but it was a huge success and even the senior officers took on their roles as pirates magnificently. The British Embassy entertained the officers and our Bluejacket Guard showed off their precision marching in the Plaza Grau, to great applause from the local population.

After a week, a little stunned by all the hospitality and official parties, we set sail, thankful for a few days normality at sea but realising why we went on these tours and how much goodwill they raised for the UK.

*   *   *   *   *

On these tours we regularly had to repaint the boat decks and forecastle every time we were to have an Open Day on board. This arduous job we completed at sea, to ensure we were shipshape at our next port of call. We also had a nightly film and various inter crew competitions.

We were now working well as a ship's company and were learning how to behave during hospitality visits. The Chilean Navy in Valparaiso offered wonderful lunches to the officers and genuine friendships grew up from these meetings, invaluable contacts in good and bad times.

We also finally learnt to sway in time to the South American maracas and keep to the beat of the drums. We were hooked by the sinuous rhythm and hooked by holding a pretty girl in your arms and whisking her round the dance floor.

Valparaiso was where the Gunroom finally got its comeuppance from the Commodore. Our trophy room of purloined signs and miscellanea was growing. We were ever on the lookout for a gem and particularly proud of the sign announcing 'The House of Intimate Things' purloined outside a ladies lingerie shop in Bermuda.

One balmy night we were wandering down a banking street in Valparaiso when we came upon a plethora of brass plates. We loved bank signs as they normally had their location printed on them. With lookouts at both ends of the street we set about removing them, when there was a little cough from above the shops. There looking down on us were local residents sitting on their balconies watching our progress. It suddenly dawned on us that perhaps our enthusiasm for this collection had got out of hand and we legged it.

Our Commodore discovered our cache and exploded with fury. We were told to get rid of every single item stored in the Gunroom mess. As we set out to sea towards the Falkland Islands, we buried our loot in the sea with formal ceremony.

We may seem like petty thieves nowadays, but in those far flung times we were encouraged to use initiative and look for adventure. We had, it must be said, taken this rather too far.

*   *   *   *   *

We were now heading further south. The weather grew colder and the wind freezing. It was a big change from the tropics and we were soon wrapped in winter oilskins on deck. There was no land, but the wondrous sight of blowing whales made up for a lack of people. We then began to see the albatross, one in particular stayed with us for days. It was bleak and cold as we turned into the Magellan Straits and the glaciers and snow-covered high country above us was truly awe inspiring.

We then arrived at the most southerly city in Chile – Punta Arenas.

The ship gave a cocktail party for both the British and Chilean dignitaries.

It was smaller than some we had given, but there was a large quantity of very pretty young girls, who came with their parents.

Our Gunroom, as usual, moved rapidly to their side and we proceeded to entertain them with our wit and erudition. One by one we were hauled by our epaulettes back from our tete a tetes, to be faced by an apoplectic Commodore. 'You will circulate!' he roared. 'You will charm the older ladies not the younger ones,' he added, ending with, 'You will learn manners on my ship.'

We all scuttled back to the party, and I often wondered what the young girls thought had happened, as we all avoided any contact with them for the rest of the evening.

At future cocktail parties we spread our charm around all ages!

We were off again to the most southerly part of our tour, the Falkland Islands.

Little did I know that in approximately 25 years' time I would be Captain of a ship heading off to fight in the Falklands conflict.

Peter in the Falklands in 1954. Little did he realise he would be back in 28 years time.

For now, I was a lowly midshipman and heading towards Port Stanley. We arrived after three days of cold windswept sailing to this rocky group of islands inhabited by sheep and penguins. There was so little entertainment in this remote place that our *We Ain't Sulkin'* was a surefire hit.

We tasted British beer for the first time in months and we all bought sheepskin rugs. We went shooting for hare and duck and walked in the hills, unlike the onboard marines who trained incessantly, as is their wont.

From the hills we looked down on San Carlos Sound, where I and my ship's company, as well as many other UK forces, would experience a real conflict in the future.

Just before we left The Falklands we took on an unexpected cargo. Our orders were to take

Penguin bound for Miami.

seven Emperor Penguins which were to be transferred to the zoo in Miami, Florida. They arrived in crates and were under constant medical supervision. They had to be hosed down with salt water every hour and were fed on herrings in tomato sauce, which they hated, as did the whole of the ship's company. These penguins were delivered safely to their onward transport six days later, and a relieved group of sailors swore they would never open a tin of tomatoes and herring again. Tomatoes were to become a recurring feature in my naval career.

∗   ∗   ∗   ∗   ∗

We arrived in Montevideo, the capital of Uruguay, just in time for the Presidential Inauguration. *Superb's* guard and Marine Band were invited to lead a full military parade in front of the new President, a terrific honour. As they swung into the square the crowd stood up and roared their approval. It was very moving and our presence did a lot of good for inter-country relations.

As per usual, both the locals and the British residents offered us overwhelming hospitality which we repaid, so it was with regret but a certain relief that we set sail for our next stop. We polished and painted everything, on our four day sea trip to Santos in Brazil.

Santos was one of the most crowded ports we had encountered. It was a mixture of the very poor and the very rich. The dock area, which contained a massive amount of shipping, was huts and swamp lands on one side and shipping berths on the other. Further into town there were the grand hotels and sandy beaches.

We went on a variety of excursions to wonderful spots like Fisherman's Island and Sao Paulo and we experienced the terrifying style of driving the Brazilians enjoyed. There were roads whose potholes were cavernous and there were speeds which Schumacher would have relished. The people were warm and friendly and the entertainment nonstop and our newfound friends came down to the shore and waved us off to Rio de Janeiro, our next port of call.

We berthed on our jetty, our moorings practically in the main street. Rio is a place of massive contrasts: wonderful beaches and huge mansions but also *favellas*, (slums) which stretch up the hills and are places of unimaginable poverty.

Although there were few official visits, we were royally entertained by the British ex pats. We were taken up Sugar Loaf Mountain and stood in awe at the outstretched arms of the iconic statue of Christ on Corcovado, overlooking Rio.

We danced the night away near the Copacabana Beach, and as usual enjoyed the warm hospitality of the Brazilians. By the time we left we were ready for some downtime.

During our nine days at sea the usual jobs ensued, painting and polishing everything into shipshape fashion.

Marching through Seattle, USA.

*   *   *   *   *

Our next stop was beautiful Trinidad – a magical island with stunning scenery and even more stunning inhabitants. We experienced steel bands and calypso music for the first time, and not one of us ever forgot its allure.

Sailing into the stunning harbour of St George in Grenada, we were a little disappointed that we had to use boats to go ashore. This limited our time and access to the delights ashore, as we had to wait for boats to pick up from the ship and the shore. We staged another Tattoo which was enjoyed by the locals and then beat a retreat on to our next port of call, Antigua.

Our trip there was extended by a small detour we took to *HMS Diamond Rock*. This is not a ship but a barren piece of rock on to which a party of sailors were sent by Commodore Sir Samuel Hood from *HMS Centaur* in 1803, to act as a small garrison and watch over Fort Royal and Saint Pierre in Martinique, during the Napoleonic Wars.

Its naming came about when Sir Samuel asked the British government to commission this rock, as a sloop, thereby giving it British sovereignty. Guns were placed there, giving the British sailors guarding it the ability to monitor shipping and keep French ships trapped in port. It was tactically brilliant, but extremely uncomfortable for the sailors left there. Sir Samuel became a Rear Admiral and continued to be one of the navy's finest tacticians.

Even today the RN expects any British naval ship passing to show its respect to the rock and this is done by sounding the Still from bosun's pipe with the ship's company standing to attention on deck.

We were only in Antigua for a couple of days, so we were not inundated with social gatherings and entertaining, but we did enjoy some beautiful beaches and some great calypso bands.

We now returned to our home base in Bermuda and had six weeks before the Admiral's Inspection. Our first test was the sea trials. This involved being taken to sea and being put through a series of problem solving and for the Admiral to see how the ship coped with them. Our Commodore had already rehearsed us with even more stringent tests, so we got through these very well.

The next stage was to ready the ship for a harbour inspection, which involved all decks and the ship to be scrubbed, cleaned, painted and polished. After a three day inspection we were ready to hear our Admiral's comments. He was delighted with both the cleanliness and efficiency of the ship and the ship's company. We had been together for a considerable time and we were a cohesive force.

It was now time to put on some regattas and sports days. *Superb* put on a very good show all round but she was particularly strong in her boat crews. I know how much we practised, as I was one of the rowers. Winning helped alleviate the muscle pain enormously.

It was time to move on now and we left Bermuda and headed towards the Panama Canal for the second time. We had all become rather blasé and only the new arrivals bothered to go on deck to see the wonders of the Canal on our return visit.

We had a couple of weeks at sea before we hit our next stop, San Diego.

This is one of the largest bases of the American Navy and the hundreds of ships lined up there made a huge impact on us. Our base was only 13 miles from Tijuana in Mexico, so the ship's company went from the USA to Mexico with ease and often, Mexico being considerably cheaper than San Diego.

American hospitality was phenomenal, particularly after we had an Open Ship Day. They showered us with invitations and we experienced rodeo shows and wonderful barbecue dining, as well as the upmarket hospitality of La Jolla. From San Diego we sailed up the coast to San Francisco.

We arrived at the Golden Gate in thick fog, so all we saw as we passed underneath this famous landmark were the supporting pillars. We berthed near the Oakland Bay Bridge and were within walking distance of the heart of the city; Market Street, Nob Hill, Fisherman's Wharf and Chinatown were minutes away.

As usual, American hospitality was generous and diverse, we in turn put on Open Days and our famous children's pirate party. The Gunroom collected chopsticks instead of signage and the ship's company made many good friends, and some less welcome ones.

I was on Watch duty and most of the ship's company had gone ashore when a middle aged lady approached the gangway. With a rather unsteady gait she walked up to me and the Officer of the Watch and, staring soulfully at me, said, 'I've come to look for a man.' She continued with a slight slur, 'I met him last night and he drinks tomato sauce, but only when he's drunk.' The Officer of the Watch told me to go and find a Chief Petty Officer and, preferably, one who drinks tomato sauce when he's drunk.

I disappeared forward and went to see the Master of Arms, who is a senior rating and in charge of discipline on the ship. Nothing went on that he did not know about.

He went to one of the messes, where he was pretty sure this Chief Tomato Sauce could be found. Once outside, he suggested that I go in and ask for the CPO and tell him the Officer of the Watch wanted to see him, adding there was no need to tell him why he was wanted.

So the CPO and I proceeded to the stern on the quarter deck, where by this time the OOW was looking very agitated as he marched up and down, followed erratically by this lady.

She was clutching a phial of some liquid in her hand, which she was taking in and out of her bag, sipping from it and then replacing in her bag. The frequency of these sips was obviously having an effect, as she became more and more rambling.

As we approached, the OOW looked up and mouthed, 'Get the police.' So I nipped away and found the liaison officer. Within minutes, sirens and flashing lights coming down the jetty heralded the arrival of the police.

Once up the gangway they looked at our female guest and with a sigh said 'Oh no, not you again!' Then turning to us one of them said, 'She escapes from the local hospital and this is her party trick. She's drinking liquid cocaine from that phial! You did the right thing to ring us, you could have had fun with this one!'

With that he looked at our guest and said, 'C'mon lady, let's go!' picked her up by the shoulders as his colleague picked her up by her feet and they proceeded down the gangplank in orderly fashion.

The CPO had beat a sensible retreat in the mayhem and we will never know if there was ever a man with a penchant for drinking tomato sauce in this lady's life.

*   *   *   *   *

From there it was 100 miles up the Columbia River to Portland Oregon. It was beautiful and huge rafts of logged wood were coming down the river as we travelled it. Portland was not a place of razzmatazz, but the people were charming. They loved our Marine Tattoo and we enjoyed beating their football team. As we left and sailed under the bridge, the lovely girls of Portland threw roses onto our serried ranks. This, apparently, is what they do if they think you're a good looking bunch. As the deck was covered in roses, I think we made the grade.

It was one day's sailing to our next stop, the naval base at Seattle. Here we received a very big American welcome. It was Seattle Sea Fair Week, so although we were not the star of the show, we were a part of it. National anthems were sung, endless speeches were made and lots of beautiful girls sang and twirled their batons to welcome us. The American and Royal Navy Open Days attracted thousands of visitors and *HMS Superb* was one of the most popular locations, so we were delighted to fly the flag, show off our Marine band and offer British hospitality.

In search of some of the beautiful girls we had seen on our arrival, a few of the Gunroom went off on an expedition into town. Not finding the girls, we drowned our sorrows and as a consequence were late back to the ship. The forward gangway was roped off at night, so everyone had to come up the quarterdeck gangway, in order that the OOW could see everybody returning as well as the state they were in.

We, in our wisdom, decided to crawl up the roped-off gangway, so that no one would notice our late return. We nearly made it. In fact we would have if the

Commander hadn't decided to go for a late night time pee. As we were congratulating ourselves on our safe return, we looked up to see his scowling countenance.

∗   ∗   ∗   ∗   ∗

Vancouver, our next stop, was in Canada, a different country but just over the Sound, so only a few miles away in reality. We had got used to the informality of the USA, but Canada was more like England.

Vancouver port is stunning, the high snow-capped mountains frame the distant landscape and the densely forested mountains behind the town add a painterly aspect to the whole vista.

We were given an official reception from the Royal Canadian naval base and we were taken on a series of tours to see Indian totem poles, the Guinness Bridge, as well as a trip up a chairlift to the top of Grass Mountain.

The Canadian Navy put on evenings of entertainment for us, and we reciprocated on board with a party and a film show.

Our next stop was in Esquimalt and the start of our journey home. We anchored outside Victoria for the night, planning our visit to the town to coincide with the RCN Regatta. We intended to win as many regatta cups as possible. We had beaten them before, but they were keen to beat us and had been in training. They were certainly bigger than us, but we were a tight team and had been rowing together for a long time in many different regattas on our tour.

We were named as the champion crew and we left Esquimalt with heads held very high.

After about three days at sea we were all looking forward to California. We anchored off shore in Santa Barbara. A local ex pat threw a huge party for us and hundreds of us went and had a whale of a time.

Our next stop was Long Beach where we docked for six days. Unfortunately, the one thing you need in Los Angeles is a car. We all felt a bit trapped without any transport, but naval training ensured that most of us managed to get by, one way or another. We saw Beverly Hills, we walked along Sunset Boulevard, some of us with a lovely companion on our arm to show us around, and we got to appreciate, through their pretty blue eyes, the real American way of life. I even met Walt Disney but he didn't offer me a starring role.

Our Tattoo yet again caused a flurry among an audience of 4000 US Marines at Camp Pendleton. We certainly enjoyed the USA and many of the ship's company had decided to return there as soon as possible. We left Long Beach and headed towards the Gulf of Mexico.

From the sunny skies in Los Angeles we were expecting sunny skies in Acapulco, but it rained continuously. Here some of us took a terrifying bus ride to Mexico City and some stayed in Acapulco.

The lure was deep sea fishing, the colourful native markets and the strolling musicians, not forgetting the exciting, if fiery foods and the inexpensive bars offering even more fiery drink. We danced in the beach night clubs, with the rain on our heads and the sea at our feet. What more could one ask for.

A royal marine subaltern was Officer of the Watch when we were at anchor off Acapulco. It was a very quiet day and the Commodore came on to the quarterdeck and threw his hat in front of him and shouted 'That's a bomb, what you going to do about it?' In best marine fashion he took one step forward and kicked it over the side. The Commodore was speechless and ordered an immediate rescue party. The quietly amused marine called out the Duty Boat whose driver happened to be me. I brought the boat round to the stern of *Superb* and trying to keep a straight face picked up a limp, damp hat and returned it ceremoniously to the ship. The marine had his shore leave stopped.

Raining still we moved on to Rodman, an American base at the head of the Panama Canal. We were there for a 24-hour stop, so most of us headed to the famous PX stores and bought the presents that family, friends, lovers and wives would expect on our return. We also took a bus into Panama City. It was yet again a city with a dual personality. The fine stores bordered the main streets, while the shanty towns were not even hidden behind them. The poor seemed piled on top of each other, with the rich so near and yet so far away. Back on board we were to enter the Panama Canal once again and for the last time.

Our journey was less tortuous and the weather cooler than before. We left the Canal and sailed for Jamaica. The Bridge was keeping a weather eye on the various hurricanes making themselves known in the area. One named *Ione* was a particular worry. We arrived in Kingston safely and then set off for our home base in Bermuda fast.

We had noticed a lack of pelicans and frigate birds in the port, and as they are normally as common in the Caribbean ports as seagulls are in the UK, we were worried. No birds in port meant that they had probably sought shelter inland and could herald a fast moving hurricane was due to arrive shortly

We sped off at 20 knots to avoid *Miss Ione* and when we had outrun her, we slowed down on the last leg of our journey to Bermuda.

In Bermuda my time with *Superb* came to an end. I was promoted to sub lieutenant and flown home, for my next appointment.

Notes

1. *HMS Superb* was a Minotaur Light cruiser also known as a Swiftsure Class Cruiser. Launched in 1944 she was scrapped in 1960.

Chapter 5

ROYAL NAVAL COLLEGE
AND HMS EXCELLENT

Once promoted to Sub Lieutenant I left *HMS Superb* and I started on a series of courses at Royal Naval College Greenwich[1] including specialist technical courses. In all they lasted about 18 months and covered a wide ranging variety of subjects.

We studied hard and we played hard. There was a healthy rivalry between the army, naval and air force training colleges. These often resulted in jolly japes very typical of the late 1950s joie de vivre.

A typical example was one night young officers from Sandhurst (Army) Royal Military Academy carried out a raid on RNC Greenwich. Swooping down in various forms of transport, they painted everything in sight bright red. Caught unawares, we were made to look very foolish the next morning when we realised what they had done.

A retaliatory move was quickly hatched and about three days later we all went down to Camberley, the town in which the Army College is situated, in our motley collection of cars. We went through the gates of the college and caused mayhem with whitewash; there was nothing that escaped the liberal dousing of the white stuff.

Having successfully completed this retaliation, we all made our way back to Greenwich. On the way home, one particular student's car came up to the traffic lights in Camberley. There was a double row of cars stationary, waiting for the lights to change, and this young naval officer thought it would be fun to paint out the windows of the cars parked parallel to him, at the lights. He got out the remnants of his whitewash and proceeded to paint the first, second and third car as he drove by. Unfortunately for him, the third car in the waiting row was a police car. A tired and angry policeman told him exactly what he thought of his prank and sent him on with the proverbial flea in his ear.

At this time I bought my first car. It was a Morris E Type, as they hadn't invented the Jaguar E Type at that time, and with the huge sum of £76 to spend I doubt whether I could have afforded the steering wheel of that car anyway.

My father's face when he saw my purchase was a picture. He sent me to a local mechanic immediately, who made it safe for a further £78. It was pale blue with a fold down hood and lacked a certain pizzazz, but it got me about and both my brothers used it until they could afford something more in keeping with their idea of cool!

My friend meanwhile had invested in a three wheeler pre-war Morgan. This could shift but was not so good at stopping. One night this car became both famous and infamous.

Around midnight, as my friend turned the car speedily into the Royal Naval College car park, the wire which operated the throttle broke and came off in his hand. He was careering out of control, and bounced off 20 cars parked there. Miraculously he was okay but he had quite a lot of explaining to do the following morning. Naturally he also had to pay for all the repairs, which made for a very poverty-stricken immediate future!

One of the greatest things about Greenwich was that it was only 20 minutes from the bright lights of London.

There were parties to go to, white tie events to enjoy and, more daring and more fun, night clubs. The singers crooned and the jazz bands jived and the smoke curled round the dimmed lights.

In those days the licensing laws were strict and police raids not unknown. If you went to a nightclub you had to dine, as well as drink. Lots of the clubs ignored this rule, much to our cash strapped relief, but the police would sometimes mount a series of raids and arrest the non dining clubbers.

One evening two of us met up with my then girlfriend and her sister. We took them to a famous night club of the non dining variety. We were all soaking up the atmosphere and enjoying the entertainment, when a sharp whistle blew and an unwelcome call rang out: 'Stay where you are!'

As the staff rushed around doling out sandwiches and the two sisters went pale the police demanded our names and addresses. The girls were horrified, their livelihood depended on a formidable aunt, who lived in Brighton. If you have ever seen the film Gigi, whose aunt controlled the purse strings and how she behaved, you have this aunt in a nutshell. She would most definitely not be amused if her nieces were arrested. Fortunately, no charges were made, but it did make us a little more circumspect in the future.

*   *   *   *   *

Having completed the range of courses at Greenwich I was sent to *HMS Excellent*[2], a land based gunnery school and the centre for ceremonial excellence. The course lasted six weeks and the Passing Out was on a very large parade ground which was the holy of holies in ceremonial terms. We survived six weeks of the square bashing course, a part of this course involving marching up and down again and again and again.

The big day finally arrived and, all ship's company and all those on the various courses were fallen in on the parade ground. Our instructors kept looking anxiously over our shoulders, as if scanning something on a distant horizon. We could not work out who or what they were looking for.

After the event, with all the marching and parading completed in orderly fashion, they let us into the secret.

A previous group of students had, unbeknown to anyone, discovered that the old First World War tank parked on the side of the parade ground still had its engine in it. Some of their group were enthusiastic mechanics and working secretly through many nights they got the old engine in working order. As the ceremonial march past began, this World War 1 tank sprang into life and shot across the parade ground and off the other side. Hanging off the tank and banging on its side were a group of instructors, but the drivers inside could hear nothing with the noise of the engine and tracks reverberating on the parade ground. This was a new addition to the usual ceremonial.

The powers that be were torn between hilarity and shock. Luckily for the intrepid mechanics the comical aspect won the day and although they did not go on leave for a very long time, the students stayed in the services and, I am sure, succeeded admirably.

Notes

1. *Royal Naval College Greenwich* RNCG designed by Sir Christopher Wren, with additions by architects Hawksmoor, Vanburgh and James Stuart. It was established as a Hospital for the support of seamen and pensioners and worked on the same principal for the navy as does the Royal Hospital Chelsea for the army. With the establishment of the benefits system the need for a permanent home for naval pensioners was reduced and the RCG became a training establishment for naval officers from all over the world. It ceased to have this role in 1998. The site has now returned to its original role as Greenwich Palace, said to be King Henry VIII's favourite residence and the birthplace of Elizabeth I.
2. *HMS Excellent* is the oldest training establishment in the Royal Navy. Located in the South west near Portsmouth on Whale Island and Horsea Island. It is both a gunnery school and a ceremonial training college.

Chapter 6

HMS ARK ROYAL NAVAL COURSE

On completion of about 18 months of courses my next appointment aged 21 years was on the aircraft carrier *HMS Ark Royal*[1]. One of my first duties as Sub Lieutenant on arrival in Gibraltar was as Officer of the Watch, which was quite good until all the Liberty men started coming back from their shore leave. We had a ships company of 3000 and they would go ashore half at a time, Watch by Watch. Because there was wine and song but no women in Gibraltar, they all drank far too much and they would come staggering down the jetty.

The Master at Arms and his team, the policemen of the ship, were at the top of the gangway and they would turn to me as each one staggered on board and say, 'Your opinion, Sir?' 'Drunk,' I'd say or 'Sober'. They were put in a place where they could recover or just totter off to their bunk.

It was quite an onerous job; those on Watch couldn't leave it at just that because those classified drunk had to be looked after. As a consequence the Petty Officer, accompanied by two assistants had to go round the bunks and check no one had swallowed their tongues which was what we were told would happen to those who were drunk. Those who had been declared drunk came up in front of the Commander the following day to receive disciplinary action which usually involved stopping two or three days leave. Nowadays they tend to hit you where it hurts and set you a hefty fine.

I had been appointed Sub Lieutenant of the Gunroom of *Ark Royal* and my job involved looking after 26 midshipmen. It wasn't that long ago that I had been one. They were a wild, marvellous bunch and we are still in contact 50 years later.

I was responsible to the *Snotties Nurse* for their wellbeing and behaviour. This strangely named person was a Lieutenant Commander and the navigator. His voice shouting down the passageway, 'Dingemans what was going on last night?' still rings in my ears; shades of *HMS Torquay* to come.

Special Sea Duty men was the name given to the most important personnel on the ship. I was the Officer of the Watch (OOW) who was one of the Special Sea Duty men. My station was OOW and the Captain made it very clear to me that should he have concern in his voice or be worried, he did not want his concern passed down to the engine room or any other controlling areas of the ship. Whatever was going on around me on the Bridge, my voice was to be calm and natural and no way to reflect the activities or language on the Bridge, whether manic or calm, to the rest of the ship. This early lesson helped me enormously during the Falklands conflict.

As a result of being OOW, I witnessed a lot of flying from the deck, both launches and recoveries (the return of plane).

My first recovery was a lesson in just how dangerous this was for both the ship's company and the aircrew. A Wyvern, a propeller driven plane was landing, but crashed and ended up in the catwalk (a passageway round the flight deck area). Its propeller broke up and sent lumps and shards of metal flying all over the deck. Thankfully no one, including the pilot, was hurt.

On another occasion a Sea Hawk recovery went badly wrong. The plane stalled on the round down (the end of the flight deck) and cartwheeled into the sea. Regrettably the pilot did not have time to exit the plane, before it sank under the waves.

At times like this, the Commander would inform the ship over the main broadcast immediately the facts were known, rather than allow rumours to circulate.

A further event happened when we were night flying and we were due to launch a number of Sea Venoms. The first one launched successfully and the two exhausts could be seen glowing in the night sky, as he climbed. The second one launched and we saw, with horror, that the exhaust flames from this plane were heading downwards towards the sea. It crashed very close to our bows. The Captain immediately ordered a change of course to ensure that the wreckage passed close by our starboard side, to avoid us ploughing through the wreckage. Unfortunately both the pilot and the observer were killed on impact.

The next event came when a Sea Venom reported that he could not get his wheels down, so we rigged the crash barrier, which was meant to stop the plane, but such was the momentum that it broke through the barrier and skidded up towards the bow. As a result of the friction on the deck, it caught fire and looked as though it was going to ditch over the bow. Luckily, he stopped three feet from the end and both pilot and observer beat the four minute mile getting out of the burning plane.

This may sound like a catalogue of disasters, but there were many more flights and recoveries than disasters. We could average 20 to 30 flights a day. The introduction of a more angled flight deck a few years later reduced accidents. However the Fleet Air Arm pilots were extraordinarily skilled but the dangers of flying off and landing on a moving ship were very real.

As another part of my job I assisted the mate of the upper deck who was responsible for the appearance and maintenance of the upper deck and the ship's side. I had a small team called the Bosun's party. We were armed with volumes of grey Admiralty paint, which we applied to cover up any wear and tear. I would take the Leading Seaman in charge in a boat and we would travel round *Ark Royal* with a china graph pencil in hand and a photograph of the ship, on which we marked the defective areas. It very much depended on how long we'd been at sea, but after a few months we became experts at knowing the likely weak spots that might need attention. If we were anchoring on an official visit, we also had to paint the cable white from water to deck.

My experience on *Triumph*, at the other end of the paintbrush, came in very useful.

I was also an assistant laundry officer. When you are washing for 3000 people, you learn a lot about washing clothes. This skill came in handy many years later when I was to realize just how dangerous washing clothes could be, in fact unchecked pockets can get you blown sky high, a story I will relate later.

Ark Royal rendezvoused with *HMS Eagle* our sister aircraft carrier which was in the Mediterranean off the Lebanon coast during one of the many crises in that part of the world. We both sat at anchor there for about two and a half weeks. At that time, the traditional rum ration had been stopped on both ships and each sailor had an allowance of two cans of beer. *Eagle* had a great big store and people would come from various areas and pick up beer for their mess.

After about a week, *Eagle's* store had ceased to be full of beer. The outside wall of boxes hid only a large hollow empty square and the beer that should have been in the centre had been purloined without anyone noticing. Some enterprising fellows had removed the hinges from the locked door and had been helping themselves to beer when they felt like it. The hinges were replaced in between forays into the store, to allay any suspicion. This illustrates the thin line between enterprise and theft, a deed difficult to replicate as it is now in naval folklore.

*   *   *   *   *

While waiting for new appointments we were often sent on a short course or to shore establishments to instruct cadets. Before I went to my appointment on *HMS Woolaston* I was sent with a group of cadets to Frimley Park[2], an army establishment near Camberley.

Once a year, a group of combined Navy, Army and RAF cadets descended on the base so that they could take part in joint exercises.

Over 200 cadets from the forces worked together and we hoped they would learn more about each other and their respective services.

There was a lieutenant or equivalent rank from each of the three services, to take charge of the operation. The cadets were divided into three groups and so each exercise was repeated three times.

The big finale of their week was to carry out a dawn attack on a hill defended by ordinary soldiers, who were part of the regular army display team.

That evening, I took my three groups, as did the other two, to the bottom of the hill where they occupied trenches already dug and in situ. The dawn attack would commence at 5.30 the following morning. The order was to run up the hill and take the enemy posts.

About 7pm that evening food was brought around, a delicious smell wafting through the trenches as it was dished out to the cadets. But nothing was on the menu for the three officers in charge. It was dry, although pretty muddy, and the three of us were hungry. My opinion of army hospitality was unprintable.

About 8.30pm I was tapped on the shoulder and a voice said, 'You're wanted at headquarters.' We were expecting to be briefed for the attack, so we rushed down there. There, laid out in splendour, was a glittering mess table, with all the glasses you would expect at a full blown dinner. My attitude to the army's hospitality did an about turn, and we three sat down to enjoy every course, with its attendant wine accompaniment.

At around 1.30am, in full tenor voice, we sang our way back to the trenches and laid our heads down to rest. At 4.40am we were roused from our slumbers to lead our cadets into battle. At the time I felt that it was not my place to lead from the front. I did, in fact, lead very quietly from the rear.

Notes
1. *Ark Royal* 1955-1979. An Audacious-Class Aircraft Carrier. Commissioned in 1955 built by Cammell Laird. First Aircraft Carrier in the world to install an angled flight deck. Scrapped 1980.
2. Frimley Park is still the Army Cadet Force Training Centre.

Chapter 7

HMS WOOLASTON

I was 22 years when I achieved my first appointment as a Lieutenant acting First Lieutenant on *HMS Woolaston*[1], a brand new minesweeper. A 'ton' class minesweeper, she and all other ships in her class were named after British towns and villages with names ending in 'ton'. She had been fitted with the new Deltic diesel engines which compared very favourably to the unreliable engines found in the previous generation of minesweepers. Trials and tests on this brand new ship started in March 1958 and the crew joined it from one of the older, dilapidated minesweepers, which was being decommissioned in Malta. *Woolaston* was most definitely an improvement.

Our Captain was a very special man, a creative and independent thinker which may not have made him a favourite with the Mandarins (the powers that be), but his spirit ensured his crew and fellow officers had a huge respect for and loyalty to him.

Woolaston's commissioning ceremony took place at Hythe, on a very foggy morning on the 4th December 1958, and the service was taken by another

The Blessing.

Ship's Company.

remarkable man, the Rector of Poole, the Rt Reverend Dr Leonard Gould, who was not only a Dr of Divinity but a highly qualified surgeon and a gynaecologist too. A very, very rare man.

He gave those assembled an inspirational service and blessed the ship, using the flat of his hand in a slow and deliberated continuous pass, along the ship's side ending this sweep with a huge cross. I can't be sure that this unusual action was special in any way but, with the benefit of hindsight, something or someone seemed to help protect *HMS Woolaston* and her crew. At just 152 foot long, she faced up to every peril thrown at her whether in harbour or at sea.

We set sail from Hythe to Gibraltar on Friday 13 December. The crew and officers wondered a little superstitiously whether it was the most auspicious day to sail.

We had been working up round the Isle of Wight and had a growing confidence in the ship and the Captain, which was just as well as the weather around the Bay of Biscay was terrible and everyone except the Captain was sea sick. We put into the Port of Brest for general repairs and then set off again for the naval base in Gibraltar.

The weather on our trip to Gibraltar was even worse and we arrived battered and bruised, feeling a little sorry for ourselves. Again a large amount of work took place repairing our communications and radar, both of which had failed.

Once these repairs were completed we started out for Malta, a thousand miles away. The sea was as calm as a mill pond when we left, and the whole ship's company was looking forward to a smooth and uneventful trip. We should have known better. This leg of our trip was going to severely test our nerves and our courage.

Early the next morning, the Sirocco (storm winds) started. The rain and wind slammed into the ship and the noise of both rose in a terrible crescendo. The sea was raging and massive waves towered steeply above us, 50 or 60 feet high, looking like giant wobbling skyscrapers. We had no choice but to keep her head to sea and trust to her seaworthiness. She was like a bobbing cork. We literally climbed one wave, only to fall 50 feet from the top of the wave, descending rapidly down into the trough, before hitting the next wave. It was like being on a nightmarish rollercoaster with no brakes, no control and no idea where or when the ride would finish.

Things did not improve when the Captain shouted above the maelstrom: 'Has everyone got a lifejacket?' The answer came back a resounding 'Yes!' but a few minutes later we realised we were missing two jackets which were stored at the other end of the ship. I and a Leading Seaman found ourselves roped together on a hazardous journey. *Woolaston* did not go through these waves she went up them and down them. Imagine climbing a mountain while the deck went vertically 50 feet up and then suddenly finding yourself hurtling downwards as the ship dropped vertically 50 feet down. We tied ourselves to anything stable on the deck, like mountaineers putting in cleats, except that our holds were heavy ammunition boxes and gun emplacements. Slowly we edged our way towards the tiller flat, where the remaining lifejackets were stacked. It took us 20 perilous minutes to get there and another 20 perilous minutes to get back. Our journey was one long prayer but we made it back on to the Bridge and delivered the jackets.

However, with the wild seas continuing to rage, on one downward plummet we hit the bottom of the wave so hard there was an almighty crack and the diesel generator stopped; as a consequence the ship lost all power. This meant we had no indication of our rudder direction, fortunately the wheel was set to full starboard rudder, so we literally corkscrewed round and round out of the wave, a truly terrifying experience. Finally, with the spare generator started and power back on, we returned to a semblance of normality. At least we knew which way to turn the wheel, as we fell off the next 50 foot wave.

Mercifully, as daylight faded we limped into the Algerian Port of Oran, physically and mentally exhausted, but grateful to be alive. Now safely berthed alongside the jetty, we watched as two huge cargo ships made port a little later. The damage they had suffered to their super structures in the same storm was considerable. Tragically, a smaller cargo ship perished in the storm. This fact brought home to us just how fortunate we had been, and what a terrific little ship, *HMS Woolaston* was. She had had her sea worthiness tried and tested and she had come through with distinction – as had we.

After a night's sleep, feeling rested and more positive, we wanted to celebrate our good luck. We had been carrying on board both general cargo and Christmas trees for the whole of the Mediterranean fleet. As reaching Malta and joining the Mediterranean Fleet before Christmas was now out of the question, we were wondering what to do with our festive cargo. Just as we were debating the question, the British Consul arrived to see what he could do to help his unexpected guests. We told him about our surplus cargo and he came up with the idea of giving them away to the local population.

At the time we thought that this was a wonderful solution. Eight taxis were ordered and the ship's company went ashore with their special cargo. Every time we saw a group of locals we stopped and presented them with a Christmas tree. The look on their faces went from surprise to amazement. In 1958 it had not occurred to any of us that not everyone celebrated Christmas. Nowadays we would be more tactful but it was meant with the best of intentions. I don't know what the recipients did with them. I doubt they were adorned with tinsel and fairy lights, but at the very least they would have made useful firewood.

However we held a divine service and gave great thanks to the Almighty for our deliverance, with honourable mention for Herd and McKenzie[2]. We finally reached Malta just after Christmas. The Commander in Chief gave the ship and her crew an Acclamation and Commendation for handling the ship so superbly in extreme weather.

*   *   *   *   *

Spain had just launched its sparkling wine, Cava, on to the international market when we had the good fortune to take part in a joint naval minesweeping exercise with the Spanish navy.

Based in Palma de Mallorca, we got on really well with our Spanish counterparts. The exercise involved all the ships from both navies sweeping the whole area for mines. We would then enjoy their hospitality and they ours, much Cava being sampled by all.

In port we were in pairs alongside the jetty. We were berthed next to another minesweeper whose Captain was considered rather too serious, and whom our Captain felt needed to loosen up.

At that time it was traditional for each minesweeper squadron to have an identifying emblem or number painted on their ship's funnels. Our squadron had identifying numbers, but our serious berthing partner's squadron had an emblem, a black foot.

Like us, all these new 'ton' class minesweepers had been fitted with the new Deltic diesel engines. When they were started up, they sprayed a fine mist of oil over the deck. In very hot weather the sailors ran around in bare feet, so within hours black footprints would appear all over the deck. This was the reason why this minesweeper squadron had designated a black foot as the emblem painted on their funnels.

Our Captain decided to give a dinner party for the Captains of all the other ships. We were told it would be a very long evening, giving us ample time to make an illicit visit to our neighbour and play a little joke on the rather uptight Captain.

As First Lieutenant I was sent with a covert group of young officers to do my Captain's bidding. All the other Captains, who were in the know, kept the party going.

Our stealthy boarding party crept on board and, finding our quarry, we painted pretty red toenails on to the previously unadorned black foot already on the funnel.

Returning to our own ship unobserved, we were relieved to see all the diners still passing the port.

The uptight Captain, as a very well trained officer, knew something was up and could no longer be beguiled to stay on board *Woolaston*. We watched him check everything on board on his return, but in the darkness he failed to notice the addition of red toenails to the single black foot embellishing his funnel.

Next morning having left the harbour, my Captain sent a message to his victim's ship: 'Hello darling!' he flashed, then all the other boats in the formation started flashing 'Hello darling' too. With great joy hundreds of binoculars were focussed on the spot. We witnessed much running around on board, but then a ladder appeared and a large tin of black paint, which resulted in the removal of the offending red toenails. No more was said.

The day before we left Palma, it was necessary to move the squadron for exercises that would take place the next day. The moves were to start at 8am, and at 7.55am, I went to the Captain's cabin as usual to report us ready to go to sea. I knocked on the door, no answer, knocked again, still no answer. I went in and he was fast asleep. Nothing I could do was going to wake him so I left the cabin and went on to the Bridge.

I announced that the Captain would not be joining us and carried on with the procedures for moving the ship to her new berth. Safely in place, I went back to the Captain's cabin to be greeted by the wonderful aroma of a good English breakfast, which he was enjoying sitting at his desk. Rather dumbfounded, I said, 'I couldn't wake you, Sir, but all is well. We are berthed in our new position.' Munching his way through a piece of toast he looked up and said, 'I had no doubt at all that all would be well.' Then he added, 'I wanted you to take the responsibility. I knew you would succeed. Now let me get on with my breakfast!'

Our Commander in Chief was given to the grand colourful gesture. Invited to visit Naples to meet his opposite number in the Italian navy, he required that a Royal Marine Band be in attendance, so that he could show off their musical prowess and impress the Italians with the glory of the British Forces.

As the budget did not stretch to flying the band and their musical instruments to Naples *HMS Woolaston* was commissioned to bring them into harbour.

We sailed from Malta and made a tremendously stagey entrance into Naples harbour, military brass band at full bore on deck, with all dressed in their best, glistening in the sunshine. This was yet another first for *Woolaston*.

*   *   *   *   *

We had a thrilling visit to Haifa the main port of Israel. The Flag Officer Middle East chose *Woolaston* as his flagship for his official visit. He was a very famous submariner, who could be very difficult. Both he and the Captain were ordered to find out as much as possible about the French built Meulari motor torpedo boats, then in use by the Israeli Navy.

Our Captain made friends with the Senior Officer of the MTB squadron, who invited him to go to sea on a trip to Acre a large sea port about 9 miles from Haifa. So with four Israeli MTB boats in arrowhead formation, at cruising speed of 40 knots, the journey began. The Israeli armed forces, though small, are one of the most efficient in the world.

Halfway there, keen to demonstrate this efficiency, the Israeli commander said: 'Would you like some air support?' 'Yes,' was the quick reply from our Captain. Support was called for and within two minutes two Mystere fighters were overhead. This was an impressive display of active capabilities.

The Admiral was so pleased with the report he brought back, that the sun shone brightly on *Woolaston* again.

At this time, things were very tense between the Turks and the Greeks, both in their respective countries and on Cyprus. The Cyprus patrol consisted of one destroyer and several squadrons of 'ton' class minesweepers based in Malta.

The main aim of the Cyprus Patrol was to police the sea to stop any nefarious actions, be it people smuggling, gun running or unauthorised landings. Smugglers worked mainly by night and from small fishing boats. Our job was to board any we thought suspicious. As most of the action took place at night, the days tended to drag by and, keeping the ship's company motivated when the work is repetitive, can be tricky.

Our Captain, with his usual flair for thinking 'outside the box', made sure that we enjoyed the hot sunshine, beautiful beaches and a sparkling sea miles from any town during the day, and we patrolled the waters by night.

Against all opposition the Captain had brought an Olympic Finn Sailing dinghy with him from the UK and had a special stage built for it on the port side of the funnel. Should we have had to go to war the dinghy would have been ditched. In one of the best morale boosting exercises I ever came across, 38 of the ship's company learnt to sail this Olympic Finn, staying fit, sharp and alert as well as having a great time.

But not content to keep morale up with the Finn, he arrived back from Kyrenia market one day with the most enormous pair of water skis. They were about four times the width of ordinary skis. As a proficient skier himself, he calculated that at a maximum speed of 16 knots *Woolaston* would make the ideal water ski boat. The skis were quite wonderful because we could tow people behind and carry out man overboard exercises at the same time. At least a dozen of us became very good skiers at the end of this period.

On another occasion the Captain took a group from *Woolaston* on a snow skiing trip in the Troodos Mountains, the highest point in Cyprus.

One lovely afternoon we anchored off a spectacular beach situated on the panhandle of Northern Cyprus. While exploring, we found giant scrape marks running from the sea up the huge sandy beach then going back down again. On closer

Captain's Finn.

inspection we discovered a very large deep hide about three feet deep. Quickly losing interest in nature studies, we moved on to the business of the day sunbathing and swimming in the sparkling sea.

The navigator was a more curious fellow; he decided on a closer inspection and eventually came across to us holding up what looked like ping pong balls. Licking his lips he proceeded to tell us how to eat them, cooked with a liberal sprinkling of pepper and vinegar. The rest of us declined this proposed treat, and we covered up the hide and returned to the ship. I must make it clear that in 1959 the turtle was not considered an endangered species. It surprised none of us that this navigator became First Sea Lord. No surprise either is that the beach is now a protected area for turtle watching. No digging permitted. Though we didn't know it at the time, out of the six officers on our little ship, two became of Flag rank (Admirals) and another Captain RN, which must be a record for any minesweeper.

One of our main assignments was to stop Colonel Georgios Grivas (who was considered a terrorist fighting for independence by the British and a freedom fighter by the Greeks) from getting arms or activists into Cyprus from mainland Greece by sea or other means. His organization, called EOKA, caused enormous problems to the British from 1954 to 1959. Colonel Grivas determined to gain independence and the British with American support determined to keep Cyprus as an important base in their fight against the Cold War.

Woolaston's job, as a member of the Cyprus Naval Patrol, was to board fishing boats to check the crew were who they said they were, and also to check they were not smuggling arms. Most of the action took place at night.

The patrol moved clockwise round the island, so we'd be in zone Alpha from 12am to 4am, then cross over to Zone B from 4am to daylight.

One boarding stays in my mind. We had stopped a fishing boat and lined up the crew who all looked identical. To a man they sported the Grivas moustache. The policeman who accompanied me on board went down below and suddenly shouted up, 'There's still one down in the hold.'

So, rather fearful, my gun in my unsteady hand and supported by one of the Able Bodied Seamen, we went down into this deep hold, where the ABS excitedly pointed to something in the corner.

'Look, there he is. There's something over there, under a blanket.'

Quick as a flash the man threw off the blanket and sat up straight in his bed. If we had been soldiers not sailors, we would probably have killed him outright. If he had been a terrorist he would probably have shot us. As it was, they went on their way and we went on ours.

Later it was discovered that some arms were smuggled into Cyprus in boxes ostensibly containing school books.

*   *   *   *   *

The Mediterranean Fleet rowing regatta was to take place on 6 August 1959, and the officers from the minesweeper squadron decided they would take part.

Captain of our flotilla was called Captain Inshore Flotilla. He was a very nice Gunnery officer – who had been the first Commander of the new Royal Yacht *Britannia*. He stated that we had no chance of winning, with the competition offered by the other ships taking part and our lack of personnel. He thought that even his ship, the frigate *Woodbridge Haven*, would beat us.

But we meant business and trained very hard. On the great day we won the prestigious cup against huge competition. Captain Inshore Flotilla was overcome. Our Captain was of course the cox.

One of the most important and you might think more light hearted jobs we undertook on the Cyprus Patrol involved the gathering of fresh oranges. These we took back to Malta at the end of our patrol time for the Admiral's wife. God help us if we returned empty handed. We didn't.

*   *   *   *   *

In 1959 politics and diplomacy finally did their work and the Confrontation and London agreement was signed, and Archbishop Makarios was to be brought back from the Seychelles, where he had been living in exile. Independence was going to be granted to Cyprus.

We were moored in Famagusta Harbour when the Captain informed me that we had been invited to a cocktail party to celebrate Archbishop Makarios' return. After the party he suggested we walk back to the harbour, catching a meal on the way.

We chose a charming Greek restaurant and ordered our meal, an abundant meze with all the trimmings. After the waiter had poured our wine, he put the bottle on the table and with a flurry of white napkins, announced loudly: 'Makarios is a mighty fine fellow!'

The Captain lifted one eyebrow, slowly swivelled round in his chair and distinctly said, 'Someone should put a big bomb up his arse!' The waiter gesticulating wildly at the other diners pointed to us with a shaking finger and proceeded to tell them what calumny had been uttered.

We got up and out as quickly as possible, with the Captain advising an Olympic-style sprint down the road. Turning sharp left, we saw another café just in front of us. Diving through the doorway, we sat down at an empty table, only to realise to our horror that we were in the same restaurant, which ran through the entire block.

This time we really hoofed it, Makarios supporters on our heels. A taxi pulled across us and our hearts sank, but the driver had recognised us as he worked in the

NAAFI. He told us to jump in and within a few minutes we were back at the ship. It was a very narrow escape.

Cyprus patrols lasted for an official 27 days. The added total of days for *Woolaston's* patrol left us short one day. That was one day short of a medal. But rules are rules in the RN. Even after we had completed two patrols we were not allowed to aggregate them and so qualify for the medal.

*   *   *   *   *

By now we had been in the Mediterranean for a year and expected to be there for the foreseeable future. The Admiralty thought differently and ordered eight 'ton' class minesweepers from the Mediterranean Fleet to the Far East Fleet, as there were no minesweepers in Singapore.

The idea of sailing with the Mother ship, *Woodbridge Haven* as one of her chicks did not warm our Captain's heart. He preferred to have more independence. Fortunately, we were, after our Cyprus patrol, in refit at the Med Fleet base in Malta, so the main group went first and we travelled with *HMS Maryton*, who was also in refit with us.

Our departure from our base in Malta was further delayed by a strike in the dockyard. The militant strikers lifted the berthing ropes off the bollards and both we and *Maryton* drifted into the middle of the basin until help arrived. We couldn't start the engines as we were both in the middle of a refit and had no power.

Captain Inshore Flotilla in Woodbridge Haven *leads the group to Singapore from Malta.*

Luckily this was their most serious action against us, although there had been threats to storm the ship, a threat we didn't take lightly. We enjoyed being autonomous and out of the orbit of the Captain Inshore Flotilla, who was now based in Singapore. He had his worries about our independent stance and disliked us being out of sight. But the day we were due in Aden was the final straw for him. We had been diverted to Djibouti in French Somalia. When he discovered our destination, a furious signal came screaming in from Singapore: 'Report forthwith, why are you in Djioubti?' Answer: 'Because there is a fuel strike in Aden.'

*　　*　　*　　*　　*

We made Bombay in good time and were well looked after by the Indian navy. Amongst the tourist events we experienced was a trip in our Captain's official car to the Towers of Silence, where the Parsees left their dead bodies to be taken up to heaven by the vultures. So, despite all the warning signs and our driver's reluctance, we drove up the hill, where a towering gathering of vultures were spiralling upwards. At this point the driver refused to go further. His decision proved a valid one when there was a sudden clang on the steel bonnet of the car and we realised with horror that a large Parsee femur, too big for the vulture to handle, had been dropped and had bounced off the bonnet. We ordered a quick return to base and the driver zoomed off with delight.

We followed on down the west coast to Colombo. When we made port we had a good rest helped by the hospitality of Ceylonese navy (now the Sri Lankan navy) and our Captain even went to call on the Prime Minister, Mrs Bandainiki.

When we finally arrived in Singapore all was forgiven and we were welcomed by the Commander in Chief's band, the end of an epic voyage for this minesweeper and her crew.

It was very hot and humid, raining every afternoon, or so it seemed. The rain was a blessing it cooled and washed our ship which lacked any air-conditioning. We had to keep our energetic Captain occupied and were delighted when he found and bought a second hand Aston Martin DB2-4 which needed a few repairs, but which kept him happy and off the ship.

He also made friends with other Aston owners, in particular a Mr Pat Thomas, a leading English business man. Along with the Wardroom's help he organised a sprint of Astons on a nearby airfield at Seleton.

Through this event we met the Sultan of Jahore who asked us to help run the Jahore Grand Prix just over the border from Singapore. Later on we flew the Sultan's flag and took him on the seafaring trip from Singapore back to the British Naval Base – a journey of around 30 miles. The Sultan enjoyed it so much we had difficulty saying goodbye to him and we were later entertained at his palace at Jahore.

Apart from minesweeping exercises we were allowed to take the ship on 'jollies' up the Malaysian Coast. On one of these we decided to have an all-day visit to a lovely bay near Port Swetenham with the whole of the ship's company, have lunch on a sandy beach, followed by an evening barbeque. We anchored very near the shore in this uncharted bay, took a line ashore in our little rowing boat and attached it to a big palm tree then, from the shore, pulled the *Woolaston* to stern into the shallows, where there were no rocks. A splendid picnic ensued followed by water sports and at sunset, always around 6pm near the Equator we held our barbeque. We had guests with us from one of the submarines and had our floodlights on.

Much later the Captain decided to swim the 40 yards back to the ship. He had not gone far, when he shouted with a savage earnestness that no one was to follow him. The floodlights had attracted the nastiest shoal of jellyfish. The poor man was lacerated with their lashing, stinging tentacles. Everyone else returned by boat. Treatment with iodine and soft water followed successfully for the intrepid swimmer!

Our visit to the Royal Thai Navy in Bangkok gave us the chance to experience an extraordinary sight. Going up the river we passed the whole of their old navy. These were moored in long lines either side of the river. There were many ex RN ships, including warships dating from 1910, it was a veritable Museum of Warships. The Thais were very friendly and after our joint exercise we were entertained extravagantly at Satahib to delicious Thai food, cabaret and dancing.

*   *   *   *   *

We played some Suzy Wong songs on our loud hailer as we entered the great harbour in Hong Kong, to be greeted by the Commodore Hong Kong and, dare I say, rather more importantly by 'Jenny's Side Party.'

This splendid Chinese lady and her band of young Chinese girls had for many years looked after and painted the RN ships sides in exchange for useful gash, cordage, soap and paint. This took all the strain of ship husbandry off the sailors, who could have a relaxing visit.

The Captain, calls completed, went to find the Aston Martin agent. On asking him for some spares for his car, he was invited to lunch at the exclusive HK Club. The agent Mr Lawrence Kadoorie turned out to be one of the richest men in the Far East, who bought one Aston Martin each year for his own and family use. He was a great philanthropist and set about making the island of Hong Kong fully supplied by farms in the Hong Kong New Territory. He also created great dams, making deep large lakes and irrigation systems which ensured they have succeeded in their great endeavour. Mr Kadoorie did not drive himself but asked the Captain if he would take him round the New Territories in the latest Aston! Whilst we were at sea in

Hong Kong waters his family looked after the Captain's wife, who was on a visit from the UK and they even took the couple sailing on his private livery junk.

Whilst there the Captain sailed his Finn Olympic dinghy in the harbour – not much fun he said, as the harbour was full of floating timbers. However, on arrival at the Royal Hong Kong Yacht Club his boat was immediately bought by a very keen member. This original purchase led to the formation of a class of Finns for their Olympics! A well travelled little dinghy.

On 25 June the Captain handed over command of *Woolaston*, and the Captain Inshore Flotilla, stated that *Woolaston* was the best of the 8 minesweepers in the Far East station. His addendum stated that her Captain had a tendency to drive it like an expensive sports car!

Notes
1. *HMS Woolaston* a brand new minesweeper built by Herd and McKenzie and launched on 2 January 1958. She became *HMS Thames*, the London RNR headquarters ship, lasting longer than any other 'ton' class sweeper. She was finally retired in 1979 still in good condition.
2. Ship builders based in East Scotland.

Chapter 8

HMS MADISTON,
LONG TAS COURSE AND HMS SEALION

I was waiting to go to *HMS Vernon*[1], a shore establishment in Portsmouth to enrol on the Long Torpedo Anti Submarine course (TAS) which would I hoped make me an anti submarine warfare specialist.

While waiting, now a Lieutenant I was appointed to command *HMS Madiston*, a brand new 'ton' class minesweeper. This was not the spectacular honour it might seem, as the Admiralty intended to rebase this and five other new minesweepers in Aden, which at the time had no minesweeping capabilities.

In fact they had no intention of letting me loose to sail their new ship. I was to be towed by RFA Royal Fleet Auxiliary *Warden*, a powerful sea-going tug. So it was a bit like being given a Ferrari without the engine. I couldn't even pretend to be driving it, as a huge wooden crate had been built over the entire superstructure covering the length and breadth of the ship, apart from some access points. Even her propellers were in boxes on the deck. The reason for all this was the baking sun in Aden. The ship had to be protected from this and the powers that be thought this the best way to do so.

The whole journey took approximately six weeks and my companions for this voyage consisted of five other members of the ship's company and one diesel generator to give us power. The tug's Captain came alongside for the passage through the Suez Canal. My presence was rather superfluous, as the rudders were locked and the propellers were on the upper deck, so my six weeks were spent reading and musing on my life on the ocean waves. On my return home I had a short leave and finally joined *HMS Vernon* for the long TAS course.

As part of this course we were expected to qualify as divers. This meant that all 21 of us on the course would go to a lake just north of Portsmouth especially built for diving training.

It has to be said that I have never much liked putting my head under water. So when we were fitted out with very smart rubber suits and a strange looking breathing apparatus, the filter of which was made up from a form of dust, I felt a definite sinking feeling in my stomach, and an even stronger certainty that I was not going to enjoy this course.

Our instructor assured us that no one had ever got dust coming through into the mask. These underwater techniques would be quite easy and safe to learn. So, with no further discussion, we were all thrown into the water and as soon as I got down to the bottom, I imagined I had dust in my mask and would shortly commence to drown. I came up fairly quickly and gave the instructor my views. He gave me a withering look, checked out my suit, confirmed there was no dust, and sent me back down again.

Later on that afternoon, we were swimming around getting used to the water, when it was announced that it was time for escape drill. They put you on the bottom, about 30 feet under, keeping you anchored there with lead weights attached to your waist. These you let drop from around your waist so, consequently, without the weights you should shoot up to the surface. The idea was that we should then be pulled ashore repeating the exercise several times to get used to it.

I do remember that the instructor did mention the importance of not forgetting to put your hand on the air indicator knob when you came up. I hated the whole of this exercise, and when he pulled me on to the shore I completely forgot to hold on to the air knob, to release the air for me to breathe. As I was pulled in I was gurgling and quietly drowning, or so I thought. The instructor and I were beginning to fall out. After being landed like a beached whale, I was less than thrilled to be told to go back down to the bottom, to collect the weights I had dropped.

He gave me some more lead weights for my waist to make me neutral and down I went. While miserably picking the previously discarded weights off the bottom, I had a serious think. This was crazy. I hated being underwater and I was pretty sure that if I continued the course, I would do either myself or someone else an injury. I decided there and then to give it up.

I came up to the surface swam to the shore and got on to the jetty. The instructors demanded to know what I thought I was doing. 'I am leaving,' I mumbled, and with as much dignity as I could muster, I dripped along the jetty away from this horrible course. I was not the most popular person. Luckily there were five others on the course who were also not up to standard.

The real agony of this debacle was that I did not receive the diving allowance of 2/6d a day. That hurt but it was better than drowning.

The officers on the Long TAS Course (1961) joined the submarine *HMS Sealion* at Londonderry where the Navigating Officer was my younger brother Norman. This is how he remembers it:

"As usual, the submarine sailed on the Sunday night to take part in a NATO exercise where the *Sealions's* task was to intercept a United States Navy Task Group that was heading across the Atlantic for the Clyde.

Patrol was established south west of Rockall and the submarine started a sonar 186 search for the task group. This required *Sealion* to be deep and slow circling so that the sonar, which comprised a series of hydrophones running the length of the submarine in the ballast tanks, and focused on the port and starboard beams, could sweep 360 degrees. The search suspended each evening and early morning so that *HMS Sealion* could come up to periscope depth to snort and charge batteries.

The next few hours were interesting as contact was held on the 186 sonar as *Sealion* increased speed to close the Task Group's track and was even held while snorting. Eventually, *Sealion* sighted the Task Group and made an approach and attack on the carrier, evading deep. In simple terms this meant the submarine avoided detection by the task group and was in position to fire on and possibly sink ships in the task group.

On return to Londonderry and as the Long TAS Course team prepared to leave Peter had to admit that some the skills and prowess claimed by submariners and his brother in particular were true. No greater compliment has ever been paid by a TAS officer to a Submariner."

Notes
1. *HMS Vernon* shore based establishment in Portsmouth specializing in training naval officers in Anti Submarine Warfare was closed and the land sold for a large commercial development.

Chapter 9

HMS YARMOUTH

After finishing the Long TAS course I was sent to *HMS Yarmouth*[1] as a Lieutenant. *HMS Yarmouth* had a problem, the boilers on board needed to run on pure water. So if the water purifying system broke down you found you were going nowhere.

We were due to join the Home Fleet on exercise in Gibraltar. Our refit in the UK had been completed and we had worked up in Portland and were ready to sail with the fleet.

We thought our water problems were resolved, but arriving in Gibraltar we discovered that we had only one gallon of pure water left. As this fault was meant to have been corrected, we were descended on by a raft of dockyard workers who tried their best to fix the fault in time for the Home Fleet exercises.

Yarmouth.

Our Captain was convinced that the problem could be rectified in time, the Engineer Officer and experts all felt he was rushing the job. As Captain it was his prerogative to set out the time frame. He refused to countenance that it was not going to be fixed properly if rushed.

The buzz went round the ship's company that it was not satisfactorily fixed, but the Captain, ever the optimist, insisted everything would be all right and any fine tuning could be finished at sea.

The following morning, looking magnificent, we backed out of the berth, turned in the bay and sailed to our given position within the Fleet formation.

HMS Yarmouth went at it hammer and tongs and we were doing well for the first hour when the dreaded call came from the engine room: 'We have dirty water!' Heads down, we limped sadly back to port in Gibraltar having only just left it in fine fettle hours before.

We berthed alongside for yet more repairs but little did we realize at the time that we were due to stay in this position for a further six weeks.

It was a sorry time. So much pressure was put on the young Lieutenant Engineer to fix the problem quickly that he was sent home suffering from exhaustion, and he wasn't the only one. The Commander Engineer was also sent home, after the constant pressure of trying to fix the fault got to him, too. It took a further six weeks to find an engineer who could rectify the problem. In that time I learnt a valuable lesson in man management, or how *not* to keep spirits up.

The dockyard would assure the Captain that everything would be sorted out within days, the Captain would tell the ship's company that we'd be off in days, and then we'd wait another week and then another. My job as Divisional Officer was to represent my chaps and I felt that they were being messed around and we didn't know what we should be doing as a ship. I remonstrated with the First Lieutenant who assured me he would do something about it.

The next morning at the Colours – the daily ceremony of hoisting the White Ensign which takes place on any ship in commission and which always started our day, the Captain growled 'Dingemans, I hear you are not very happy with the way I'm running the ship.' I thought to myself, here comes big trouble and thank you very much First Lieutenant. With a gulp, I said, 'Sir, you say one thing, but the rest of ship knows it's not possible. It makes people very uncertain, Sir!' I have to say he had the grace to listen to me and to take on board that I meant no disrespect, I didn't have to walk the plank and we set sail from Gibraltar six weeks later.

*   *   *   *   *

The Royal Navy performs a lot of official visits to allied countries and navies. This time we had been invited to Amsterdam. The general form on these occasions was for the Captain to go off and exchange pleasantries with the local Mayor or Council, who would then return his call and, once those formalities were over, we were free to play a lot of sport.

On this particular visit, the local golf club, a very famous one, asked us if we would like to play and have some lunch. We naturally accepted with alacrity. None of us were very good players but we were keen. As the senior Lieutenant I was given the job of leading the group off and given the honour of hitting the first ball. I prayed as I addressed the ball on the first tee and I smacked it right down the middle of the fairway. It was a most extraordinary freak shot and got much applause. We could do no wrong and balls were hitting the greens, bunkers were avoided and putts were dropping perfectly. The problem was, of course, that it is not accepted protocol to beat your hosts. The Dutch team who had not expected to lose did not look happy!

It didn't cause an international incident, however, as things changed rapidly after the first round. The reason for this was the stop for lunch – a very, very long lunch. We arrived back at the first tee for the second round at around 3.30pm. We staggered on to the course and they wiped the floor with us.

Notes

1. *HMS Yarmouth* was a Type 12 Frigate Rothesay Class. Built by John Brown & Company and commissioned in 1960, she was used as target practice in a naval exercise and sunk in the North Atlantic in 1987. NB. The famous *HMS Hood* also had a problem making pure water. She only just made it back to the safety of Scapa Flow on one occasion as all her pure water had run out. She was of course the ship, which attacked many German warships, but was tragically sunk by very accurate German gunners on the battleship Bismark.

Chapter 10

HMS RALEIGH

After my time at sea on *HMS Yarmouth* I was put in charge of a leadership course based at the shore establishment *HMS Raleigh*[1] in Plymouth. It was a very tough course. Both instructors and students would go out on exercise to the moors, deep into the countryside and along the coastline each weekend. In these locations the students were given lots of tasks from map reading to a variety of challenging adventures to test their abilities, their leadership skills and to teach them to cope under stress.

I and my staff would drive around in a nice warm Land Rover and watch the students struggle through the tasks set for them. It should be noted that we had taken the trouble to get the balance right on this course, and we did not ask the students to do anything we had not completed successfully ourselves. It certainly sorted out the men from the boys.

Bodmin Moor.

While the students faced the challenges of sleeping in tents on Bodmin Moor, we had an arrangement with owners of the famous Jamaica Inn, allowing us to sleep there, in the stables. They fully expected us to have a few pints beforehand in exchange for their hospitality suite, a burden we found easy to carry. For a year I slept in the spooky Jamaica Inn for one night, every month. We saw the students walk along the smugglers paths to and from the moor, but to my disappointment we never saw a real or ghostly smuggler in the Inn.

The students were not the only ones feeling shattered on this course. In my cosy Land Rover I carried a large circular box in which we kept the thermos of hot tea that kept our spirits up in the dark windy night. This was a very effective piece of equipment as it really did keep the tea hot, unlike many thermos where you get a lukewarm brew.

I would take this home with me to refill for the next challenge after the night's trials were finished. The chaps always dropped me home after the exercise, as I lived near the base. Before waving them off one night I put down this heavy box with the precious cargo and failed to notice how close to the wheels it was. As the chaps backed up there was a tremendous crunch, and thousands of shards of glass lay glinting in the moonlight, decorating the driveway.

This course reignited my love for the navy and I had a real urge to go back to sea again. My luck was in as my next appointment was my very first command *HMS Maxton.*

Notes
1. *HMS Raleigh* is a shore based establishment in Plymouth where all new ratings receive basic training and development in leadership skills.

Chapter 11

HMS MAXTON AND RAF BRACKNELL

I was given my first command in 1966. I joined *HMS Maxton*[1] as a Lieutenant Commander in Plymouth, immediately after her refit. During her refit she was converted from minesweeper to mine hunter. She was dressed in new lightweight armour which added strength to her hull and an additional gun gave us much needed extra firepower.

HMS Maxton was involved in a collision with another vessel before I took command. While on the Cyprus patrol there were two adjacent areas policed by a frigate and a minesweeper (*HMS Maxton*). They exchanged zones every two or three

Maxton *at Speed.*

hours to create different patterns for those searching and those watching. It was dangerous moving from one zone to another especially as all ships were blacked out to avoid being seen by the Cypriots.

This type of patrol can be very boring. On board the frigate, the Operations Officer and the Officer of the Watch suggested they do some interception to liven

Stern view.

things up a bit. There was no thought of danger and they saw no reason to consult the Captain.

The Operations Officer remarked, 'I've picked up something on the radar about three miles ahead, it looks like a bit of floating wood. Let's try a cutting out exercise.'

This involves the ship passing over the object at speed.

It is now time to change perspective and see things from the point of view from the Officer of the Watch on *Maxton*. What he saw was this frigate passing close down the side of them and just missing them, from about a cable astern.

Back on the frigate, the Officer of the Watch shook his head ruefully and said, 'Blast I've missed it! Let's go and have another go.'

The frigate turned and charged full steam ahead towards *Maxton* and hit her bang amidships. Not a piece of wood then.

One of the sailors sleeping on *Maxton* was propelled out of his bunk through the mass of paint, stored in the forward part of the frigate for safety reasons, and landed on the bow of the attacking frigate, naked but for a liberal covering of battleship grey and camouflage green paint!

Maxton limped back to the UK for a full refit and modernisation. I can't tell you what happened to the Officer of the Watch on the frigate.

When I took over as Captain you could still see the damage on the starboard side although it had been properly repaired. The thought of the paint-spattered sailor stayed in my mind.

When I took *Maxton* to sea for the first time, it was a thrilling moment. She had carried out all her trials alongside successfully, but we needed to test all elements in sea trials before she was declared fully worked up.

We sailed from Plymouth and everything seemed to go smoothly and be in good working order. She responded nicely and was easy to manoeuvre as she was fitted with active rudders. Each rudder had an electric motor mounted on it and would turn through 60 degrees. This enabled the mine hunter to run on active rudders only, and she could turn on a sixpence when hunting, which ensured she could avoid any mine-like objects on the seabed. These rudders were controlled from the Bridge. They are quite a common form of equipment in these ships. We also had fitted a new Bridge controller for the main engines. This was a sort of cabinet with two handles and you turned these from the Bridge, rather than having to give verbal orders to the engine room to stop. The principle of course was that those on the Bridge had complete control of both the engine and the active rudder.

At the end of the first day's sea trials, we were coming up to my very first berthing alongside in my new command. We executed quite a good approach and I got a head rope out, so I was secure. Turning to the Chief in charge of the engine control handles I said, 'Slow ahead port, slow astern starboard.' As he turned the handles to carry out

Buccaneer plane.

my order, he turned to me and with a rather stunned expression on his face and, panic in his voice, he said; 'Sir, one of the handles has come off in my hand.'

My first command and I was unable to control the ship. I suspect the look on his face mirrored my own. I realised it meant we now had only one engine doing what we wanted it to do, but we eventually came alongside.

With the benefit of hindsight, and a lot more experience, we should have cut one engine, and used the active rudders.

But I'll never forget the look on the Chief's face when he looked down at the handle in his hand and I don't think he will ever forget mine either!

Just after this incident we received orders to proceed on a search mission.

Amongst our basic armaments was the mine hunting sonar, which would send a sound beam down to the seabed. On contact with an unidentified object the beam would bounce of it, creating a shadow sent back to our onboard screen. It was then up to us to decipher what the shadow resembled – as a mine hunter we were generally searching for mines. Divers would be sent down to check any suspicious object. If it was a mine they would destroy it, if it were something innocuous and harmless they would simply write a report.

While still doing my sea trials before setting off to the Far East, we received a message from *HMS Victorious* which was nearby. One of the new Buccaneer planes had been launched from the carrier and had crashed in the sea. We were directed to the scene to try and detect the plane. It was in the early stages of development so it was important to find out what had gone wrong.

The normal depth we worked at was 180 feet, so we hunted in four ten-mile squares round his point of entry with the mine hunting sonar, and monitored the screen. After three days' seeking we were coming to the end of the search time allotted. I was beginning to believe we would not find the aircraft when suddenly the operator yelled, 'We've got something!'

There, on the screen, at about 360 feet, well over our normal search depth, was the Buccaneer, you could not mistake the very distinctive tail shape.

When we found things, we normally marked the spot by mooring a small rubber dinghy above the position. This time we had to rig up a buoy big enough to be seen by the large contingent looking for it. We were pleased that our first mission was a success. The crew of the Buccaneer had ejected and were quite safe.

After sea trials we headed for the Far East and passed through the Suez Canal. Most of the time we sailed on our own but were sometimes joined by other ships for a short passage. On our trip down the Canal we had no escort.

Maxton *with mine hunting equipment on display.*

We had been told to keep a close eye on the aircraft along the Suez Canal and report back to the MoD on any unexpected planes or a build-up of forces.

My intelligence team was briefed and when we stopped to pick up the Egyptian pilot who would accompany us through the Canal we were even more surreptitious in our spying. As we were passing down the canal we saw our first airfield. A small cough behind me made me turn and the pilot spoke as follows:

'Sir, as you seem so interested in our planes let me tell you there are three Migs, three Transport Aircraft and eight more Migs coming back tomorrow. We have nothing to hide.'

With a small bow and a smile he carried on directing our route down the Canal.

Just before he disembarked, he turned to me again and solemnly and with pride addressed the Bridge: 'No one thought we had the skills to reopen the Suez Canal, but we did. We are a proud people and we were determined to prove ourselves to the World.'

With that he left the ship and left us a little wiser.

*   *   *   *   *

A ship from the Royal Auxiliary escorted us from Aden to Cochin in case we met any navigational problems. It was also needed to refuel us for our onward trip.

Our arrival in Cochin had been signalled forward to the Indian navy. Someone had muddled the signals and instead of being the lowly Lieutenant Commander I was, I suddenly evolved into a four-stripe Captain. He would be treated as a VIP and I wasn't on the red carpet just yet.

The Commander of the naval base came on board and said that, despite their mistake, they'd stick to the programme they had arranged for my four-stripe Captain entertainment. This meant a magnificent series of parties and events, including the Cochin equivalent to the Oxford and Cambridge boat race. Crowds lined up to cheer

Sheraton *on passage to Japan in rough seas.*

Officer of the Watch manoeuvres.

the two heavily laden boats while 60 rowers on each boat battled it out. It was an unexpected, but fascinating five days. A taste of things to come, I hoped.

＊   ＊   ＊   ＊   ＊

After her refit in the UK *HMS Maxton* was bristling with armour plating, new guns and new communication systems, all ready for active service in the Indonesian conflict. The day I arrived in Singapore, the conflict was over, the UK ended up with a surfeit of ships out east and many were sent home or re-located. But two squadrons of minesweepers were to be kept in the area.

I have very fond memories of one particular trip to Bangkok with the whole of the Flotillas, 25 ships in all.

The Captain Inshore Flotilla would sit down to a lovely dinner then, well dined, would go on to the Bridge and do Officer of the Watch manoeuvres. These involved the ships rotating their positions while being watched on radar screen. It was reminiscent of a mad *Dashing White Sergeant.* We went round and round, crossing over and behind, back and forward.

Maxton would go from position 50, to position 100, but four other ships would be doing the opposite. It meant a very hairy night and we always got a leak from the

Flag Ship to announce when the Captain Inshore Flotilla had finished dinner, so we could ensure he witnessed a carefully choreographed exercise.

As long as you got your ship through the gaps and he could identify you on the screen, no one minded too much where you were. How there were no collisions I will never know, but it was superb training in developing the Commanding Officer for the big warships of the future.

Every three months or so, a pair of minesweepers would come up from Singapore and do guard duty around Hong Kong island so that the Chinese could see it was not completely undefended. At this time about 11 minesweepers were on exercise in the area.

During this exercise, the weather was bad and the Chinese were threatening to cut off the island's water supply. They had also threatened to sail through the harbour flying the Chinese flag. At the time we had been running a successful compromise, whereby the Hong Kong fishermen had to have a licence, granted by the British and the Chinese authorities, to come into the harbour.

We received information that a flotilla of fishing boats were sailing in formation towards us in the harbour. The Chinese authorities had recently recalled the Hong Kong fishing fleet, ostensibly to check their licences, and then had instructed them to sail in strict formation through Hong Kong harbour flying the Chinese flag. The Governor decided to call their bluff and sent ten minesweepers to break them up. The minesweepers, with much assistance from local fishermen did the deed.

As the single minesweeper left guarding the colony, I was summoned to the Governor's office, where I was given authorisation to open fire on any Chinese incursions. These would be warning shots across the bows, but with my one gun to defend our honour I did not relish being the defender of British pride. I am glad to say a showdown was averted and Hong Kong continued to thrive under the Union Jack for a few years to come.

After this little confrontation, four of the sweepers were sent to Borneo to practice sweeping in a location that was considered a probable area of future confrontation.

Sweeping involved travelling into the minefield trailing a long wire on which there were cutters and a float which held the wire up. The mine slid down the wire into the cutter and then bobbed up to the surface; you would then destroy it with machine guns. We were in quarter line one, two, three, four ships and the number four got her navigation wrong and ran into shallow water and then aground. The first indication of trouble to the rest of us was when we heard the signal: 'Mayday! Mayday!'

Each ship had to haul in our wires, which took a little time. We then returned to help her.

The form, if you run aground in the RN is to lighten the load, by throwing everything movable overboard. By the time we got there, everything was being thrown overboard and great lumps of metal were splashing into the brink, including the kitchen sink. When the tide went out, we could see she was resting on the bottom, holed by a huge lump of coral. We floated her off and towed her with our sweep wires to safety. It was a great seamanship lesson for us all. Going aground is a nightmare which haunts every naval Captain. The reporting of items 'lost at sea' increased rapidly.

*   *   *   *   *

While stationed in Singapore most of the ship's company including myself either had visits from their family or had their family based in Singapore.

Once a year we had a family day, when we took the ship's crew and their families to a beach and had barbeques and family fun. This was a great way of keeping up spirits and getting to know the wider family on board.

It was a very relaxed day and I had one of my sons perched on my lap as we journeyed down the Straits. Suddenly the ship veered to the right heading straight towards a sandbank. 'Run aground' on my ship was not in my vocabulary so my son was sent hurtling through the air where a sailor caught him in a magnificent running catch. I meanwhile corrected the problem and we continued on our way.

What happened to cause this sudden lurch was never discovered, but we guessed a floating piece of wood may have been the cause. Poor *Maxton,* planks of wood did not agree with her.

*   *   *   *   *

Our flotilla made an official visit to Bangkok, where a most enjoyable time was had by all. We were invited to a garden party in the British Embassy gardens where I heard this fascinating story. In the centre of the gardens, but visible from the road, a large statue of Queen Victoria dominated the surroundings. The Thais had decided this statue was a fertility symbol and if a Thai woman wanted to become pregnant she would look into Queen Victoria's eyes, and nine months later, her wish would come true. The Japanese, when they captured Thailand in 1941, decided to cover Queen Victoria's statue with a huge tarpaulin as they considered it a symbol of Imperial tyranny. There were so many complaints from the local population, that the Japanese were forced to cut a small square in the covering tarpaulin so the Thai women were still able to look in her eyes.

The day before our departure from Bangkok I was instructed to go ahead and prepare for an exercise, my role being the enemy. I was to await the arrival of the main body of the flotilla. Meanwhile I was given a pilot to guide me down the river and into the sea.

The channel from the river to the sea was badly buoyed and stretched over five miles into the distance. Those on the Bridge, especially the navigator and me, became increasingly worried by the advice being given by our pilot. I asked him, 'Do you know where we are?' and he replied with a shake of his head 'No.' I looked at the echo sounder which was an uphill slope from 30 feet to three feet. We were very nearly aground but we managed to avoid the grounding and got back into the right channel. We couldn't wait to drop the pilot back to his boat, when we finally made it safely to sea.

With my first command under my belt, my next appointment was once more on shore. I was sent to the RAF Royal Airforce Staff course at Bracknell.

Two of the services sent three students on this staff course and all were Lieutenant-Commanders or equivalent rank. There were two Royal Navy officers and one Royal Marine. There were also three army officers. Apart from these the rest were all RAF officers. Our first experience of a different service lifestyle was when we three went to the bar at lunchtime, for a nice gin and tonic that was the naval way – only to find that the bar was empty. The custom in this establishment was to go home for lunch. Drinking at lunchtime was not the norm, so it was a sobering experience for us and remained so throughout the course.

The standard of teaching was extraordinarily high. They assumed we were all idiots and we started with pronouns, adverbs and then moved on to colons and past participles and finally built up to an understanding of English grammar. By the end of the course, we were very well trained to write the letters or the papers expected from senior officers. We were also thoroughly versed in how to control air movements and direct bombing, where appropriate.

Notes

1. *HMS Maxton* a minesweeper named after a village near Edinburgh. Built in 1956 by Harland & Wolff she was converted to a minehunter in 1966. She was scrapped in 1989. She was the only ship called Maxton in the Royal Navy. (The lessons learnt from the 1963-1966 confrontation with Indonesia were used by naval planners to ensure that the problems with equipment and ships discovered then, were rectified.)

Chapter 12

HMS TORQUAY

I joined *HMS Torquay*[1] as a First Lieutenant, with the rank of Lieutenant-Commander. *Torquay* was a Dartmouth training ship and, as such, we followed the same itinerary as I experienced in my previous incarnation as a midshipman on *HMS Triumph* and *Vanguard* – The West Indies in the winter, the Mediterranean in the spring and the Baltic in the summer. The Officers of these training ships were chosen for their ability to set an example and ability to train and educate, at the same time following the Captain's orders. And as First Lieutenant I was very lucky to have a good and kindly man as Captain.

On one occasion four ships berthed on the jetty in a two by two formation. The Senior Officer was alongside the jetty with *HMS Torquay* berthed alongside her and the other two ships berthed astern. It was the Gunnery Officer's birthday. He'd been ashore and had obviously had a pleasant evening. I'd been on duty, so when he came back, my duty completed, I said, 'Ben it's your birthday, we must celebrate!' And with these words, our group of young officers produced some champagne and continued to celebrate his birthday for a considerable period, demolishing several bottles to the cause.

Torquay.

Ben, being a gunnery officer, said in that focussed manner of the well oiled, 'I must see if I've lost any of my targeting capabilities.' So, with infinite care, he picked up a champagne bottle and threw it across the wardroom, through the porthole and with unerring accuracy it smashed against the side of the ship to which we were berthed.

Ben repeated this action five times with the same accuracy. After that, we persuaded him that it was quite an achievement as it stood and further proof of his capabilities were probably unnecessary.

However, the next morning the Captain of the squadron sent for me as I was First Lieutenant and asked rather wearily, 'Now then, Dingemans, what was all that racket about last night?'

'Well, Sir,' I said with what I thought was pretty quick thinking, 'we were having gunnery practice and we were proving that the accuracy exercise could be effective both late at night and early in the morning.' With a theatrical sigh the Captain looked me steadfastly in the eye and replied, 'This is not to happen again,' and with an even bigger sigh, he added, 'But it probably will.'

*　*　*　*　*

The First Sea Lord was about to retire and our ship was chosen as the perfect location to host a farewell to himself and his wife. These retirement farewell parties were to take place in London and we duly sailed up the Thames and moored by Tower Bridge. I have to say we glistened. There was not a patch on the paintwork or bloom on the brass. My Buffer, the senior seaman on board, who was responsible for the cleaning and who was very much a man of the old school, always had a bosun's pipe on his person as well as a pot of green paint and a pot of grey. Just before anyone arrived, he would go round with his touch-up pots to make sure everything was spick and span.

The retiring First Sea Lord had a disabled wife and as she came alongside in a naval launch we were ready to swing her aboard. The Buffer whistled instructions on his bosun's pipe, a tweet here and a tweet there. It was a textbook transfer and had the charm of yesteryears.

Both the Admiral and his wife were enchanted by the manner in which she was brought on board.

Our mooring at a buoy just below Tower Bridge meant that our departure involved quite a tricky manoeuvre. There was quite a tide running and the Captain had to take the ship towards the centre of the river then turn it to head down river. We decided where I was going to be positioned so that we could have constant eye contact.

First Lieutenants and Captains soon develop a silent rapport with each other so they can do things without having to refer verbally to each other. In this case we had just turned and my Captain looked at me and I nodded, which was my way of saying all was fine. Suddenly, one of the ship's company rushed up to me shouting, 'Fire! Fire! Fire!' apparently in the engine room. I immediately informed the Captain and went down to the engine room to check it out. A pipe had broken and was spilling oil into the engine room right under an exhaust fan. This normally allowed warm air from the engine room to exit onto the upper deck in discreet warm puffs. There was nothing discreet about the smoke exiting the engine room this time. Our shiny glistening ship sailed down the Thames emitting a plume of black dirty smoke. Not quite the departure we had in mind.

Notes
1. *HMS Torquay* a Type 12 Whitby class frigate. Built by Harland & Wolff. Commissioned 1956 she was the longest serving frigate in the navy before she scrapped in 1987. She served in Suez but later played an important part in training young officers.

Chapter 13

FAR EAST AND THE MINISTRY OF DEFENCE

After finishing on *Torquay* I was sent out to the Far East as the Staff Warfare Officer to the Flag Officer 2nd Flotilla, the seagoing Admiral in the Far East. We were a very small staff who were constantly on the move. Our role involved flying the flag or taking control of the various operations and exercises across the whole of the Far East. One minute we were in Australia, the next in Japan. It was a fascinating time as a great technological breakthrough in the detection of submarines had been made. It was called passive sonar, and allowed us to pinpoint both friendly and enemy submarines without them pinpointing us. Formulating exercises that would test this new system was stimulating and exciting.

I was on duty with another member of staff over Christmas and we were writing the orders for the big annual exercise that took place in the New Year. At about 8pm I said, 'I've had it now, I'm going to have a shower and a drink.' My colleague said he would follow shortly. I had just got under the shower, when he rushed in and shouted 'Peter, you've been promoted!'

At that time, at the end of each six-month period a list of people who had been selected for promotion from Commander to Captain, or Lieutenant-Commander to Commander was published and was posted around the whole navy. It had arrived in my absence.

'Are you sure it was me? I have a brother it could be him.' I was always pretty sure he would beat me to promotion.

My colleague rushed away and came back a few minutes later: 'Are your initials PGV?'

I nodded, a smile forming on my face. 'It's you then!' he said, with a reflecting grin. It was the best Christmas present to date! I was promoted to Commander.

Note from my Appointer: "You were selected earlier than I thought, so you will have to come back from the Far East."

I had apparently surprised my appointer. It is his job to ensure that the best officer is chosen for every job that comes up. It is important for officers to spend time in an appointment in the MoD if they want promotion. The Appointer chooses the best officer for a particular job. He recommends his selection to the Naval Secretary who approves all appointments. Officers visit their appointer every few years. For higher ranks the Naval Secretary puts forward the selection to a board of Admirals.

*   *   *   *   *

Much to my delight my first posting as a Commander was to the Ministry of Defence.

My job was working in the Directorate of Naval Plans and I experienced a huge learning curve. They were a very stimulating and thought provoking two years. Our department was responsible for naval deployments everywhere west of Suez and we were also in charge of worldwide maritime strategy.

At the end of this time I went before a selection board chaired by an Admiral. The RN uses this process of selection to decide whether you are suitable to be in command of a ship or would be more suited to a desk job. They want to assure themselves that you are capable of commanding a ship worth millions of pounds. If you convince them of this, you are then sent on a series of courses for about six months, which aim to bring you up to date for the type of ship you have been given. Much to my delight I was selected for a command at sea. This meant that I was entitled to some home leave and gave me a chance to catch up on the domestic front.

The powers that be said, 'Peter, take a good long leave and we'll fix some courses up for you when we know where you're going. We'll ring you in a few months.'

I got home and started to relax. On the following Monday morning, I got a phone call. 'Peter are you there?' 'Yes,' I said, laughing at my short holiday. 'Where do you want me to go?' 'Gibraltar. We've just removed the Captain and the First Lieutenant of *HMS Berwick,* the ship is in a parlous state. We'll get you the best replacement First Lieutenant available and you can both get down there and sort things out.'

Chapter 14

HMS BERWICK, HMS LOWESTOFT, HMS SEALION AND THE MOD

We flew straight down to Gibraltar and were shocked at what we found. I had never seen anything like it. This ship, the frigate *HMS Berwick*[1] my ship was now, to put it kindly, very crabby indeed.

A Royal Navy ship is painted battleship grey. This one looked as though someone had used up all the dregs in the old tins of paint they had had lying around, which were, unfortunately, at least six different shades of grey. She looked like an old

Frigate refuelling.

tub in bad camouflage, not a ship of Her Majesty's Navy. The ship's company showed no pride in the ship, and in the previous couple of days, before our arrival, something mysterious had appeared on the previous First Lieutenant's bunk. It had been covered with a large pile of gash (rubbish).

There had been and still were some other very strange things going on. Some unknown trickster was illicitly switching off machinery. He was an irritant rather than a danger at present, but these kinds of actions can develop into serious dangers for the ship's company.

We thought we knew who it was, but we could find no proof. We just had to keep a watchful eye on all machinery and the suspected culprit. From Gibraltar we headed towards Scotland. The First Lieutenant and I gave both the ship and crew a thorough work up on the way, but morale had sunk so low that it was difficult to motivate the crew.

One moment of relief from the constant pressure to improve the ship's company came when my brother met us on an RV in the Bay of Biscay. His submarine *HMS Sealion* had just completed a naval exercise and was en route to Gibraltar. Ships on exercise exchange records on the completion of an exercise, so that they can compare and check actions to see whether they could have improved their own performance.

As *Sealion* surfaced all the men on the upper deck of the Bridge on *Berwick* were very smartly dressed ready to watch the transfer of records and were pretty taken aback when the submariner officers appeared wearing a truly motley collection of outfits. I believe my brother, the Captain, was wearing a coloured shirt and khaki shorts. Submariners have a much more casual dress code and avoid wearing their uniforms as the heat and cramped conditions ruin them.

Despite my determination to insist on a smartly turned out crew and despite being undermined by my own brother, the First Lieutenant and I continued to push *Berwick's* ship's company hard to try and build up teamwork and a pride in the ship.

This had taken a big blow when *HMS Berwick* had been sent packing in disgrace from the formal Fleet work ups in Portland earlier that year, a heinous crime in the Royal Navy.

Despite our hard work, as we headed towards Rothesay to act as Guard Ship to the Clyde Regatta week, I don't think I have ever been so ashamed in my life. We had tidied her up as best we could, but we didn't sparkle, as warships are meant to sparkle on these occasions.

Faith, my wife, came up to Scotland and we stayed in a hotel ashore. On the last night before we headed off for the Icelandic Patrol, I was happily dreaming of the delicious smoked haddock I would be sampling for breakfast the next morning, before I rejoined the ship about 9am.

Instead I was rudely awakened by a phone call at 4am saying, 'Sir you better come quickly, we've found sand in some oil filters.' This was just what we did not need.

I had a very good engineer who, against all odds, got the engine started so we could crawl up into the submarine base and moor alongside their jetty. The engineers from Faslane turned up in force, brilliant in an emergency, as always. We were back up and running in hours.

We never did catch the saboteur. Our guess was that the sabotage was being used as a spoiler, aimed at delaying or stopping our trip to Iceland. Once it was inevitable we were going, the saboteur gave up and we had no more trouble.

With all systems working well, we set off for Iceland, our job to protect our fishing fleet from being harried or having their lines cut by the Icelandic navy. These were the early patrols, the beginning of the so-called cod wars and both the Icelandic navy and our RN had not yet got the measure of each other. They had a box of tricks they brought out to test the new boys and thoroughly enjoyed using them. On our arrival, they would have one of their highly manoeuverable mini boats waiting inside their territorial limits, for an opportunity to test our mettle and disrupt our fishing fleet.

It was foggy and visibility was partially obscured when we came up towards the edge of their coastal waters, the 12-mile boundary. As we moved into our protection position for guarding the UK fishing fleet, one of my crew suddenly shouted 'Radar contact, Sir,' and there on the screen was a fast moving object coming from their territorial waters and hurtling towards us. The mist cleared and we identified one of their specialist mini boats sent out to annoy and test me.

This is what I was in the RN to do. We spent the most exhilarating half hour, backing and filling in the frigate, which is not designed to turn on a sixpence and I managed to keep them away from the fishing fleet for 45 minutes. At one point, I thought they were going to get past my stern and head for the fishing fleet, so to let them know I really meant business, I ordered the engine room to go full astern. If their small boat got in the way of a frigate going full astern, it was too bad. These actions had the desired effect. They headed home.

The fishermen thought I was the best thing since sliced bread. Not only did we succeed in protecting them from further Icelandic harassment, we only had one line cut during my tenure.

It was also terrific to see that those on board the ship were now working as a proper crew and morale was high. Success breeds success.

We had completed our patrol, kept our fishing boats safe, so we had reason to be proud of the ship and her crew on our return to Plymouth. The First Lieutenant and I had thought long and hard about this homecoming. The Flag Officer of Plymouth was the Admiral who had given *HMS Berwick* the thumbs down in Portland and sent her off in disgrace under her previous command.

We decided on a rather radical move. We'd paint the ship at sea. This is not an easy task at the best of times, but we decided to stop off mid ocean, put men over the side so that they could work from shipyard-type platforms. A small boat would drop them alongside just under the platforms, so they could paint right down to the water line, and then pick them up when they'd finished. It was a logistical nightmare but the madness of the scheme appealed to us all. We painted that ship from top to bottom and bow to stern. By the time we'd finished I have to say she sparkled. In fact, we all did.

When we went into Plymouth, I think the Flag Officer Plymouth nearly fell off his chair. I had signalled earlier, saying; 'I hope you won't mind me asking you to review the ship, in view of its past history.' He came down to the ship and took me aside at the bottom of the gangplank with a quick nod in the direction of *Berwick*. He asked, 'How are things with you?' I replied with, I admit, a lump in my throat, 'They are just fine, Sir. You can be proud both of your ship and your ship's company, as they and I are proud to be on this ship.'

He went down to the quarterdeck where the whole of the ship's company was assembled. You could see that there was a huge wave of trepidation among those lined up for inspection and the Admiral presented them with a very dour face. Then miraculously, a huge smile broke out over his face and he said with real pride in his voice, 'Well done *Berwick*! You've shown you can do it. I'm very impressed. Now keep it up.' It was quite a moment for us all.

After our success in the regeneration of *Berwick* and her ship's company, she was due a refit. This refit was to take place in Gibraltar. My orders were to take *Berwick* to Gibraltar and then transfer her crew to *HMS Lowestoft*[2] a frigate which had just completed her refit there.

On arrival, I asked my specialist heads of department to visit *Lowestoft* and report on the standard of the refit. They all came back with bad news. There was an enormous amount of work to be completed which would fall on our shoulders, letting the dockyard off the hook. The work that had been completed and signed off was sub standard.

After the discussions with the Commander in Chief staff, I said that I was not prepared to take an incomplete ship and the dockyard would have to complete it properly. They supported me, and I called on Flag Officer Gibraltar and told him I was not prepared to take *Lowestoft* until she had been brought up to the requisite standards.

He said, 'You cannot do that, you must take her.' But eventually The Flag Officer could see that nothing would change my mind and accepted that *Lowestoft* should remain in dockyard hands, until the work was complete.

We finally sailed home, but on arrival in Portsmouth another six weeks' work were required to sort out the gunnery system. A few months later I handed over a good ship to my successor and moved on to other challenges.

In fact it was back to a second stint at the MoD. This time I became a member of the Joint Services team. Our job was to work across the services and my tenure came just after the joint defence cuts had been decided. It was our job to deal with these cuts and put them into practice. I feel for those doing the same thing as I write.

Notes
1. *HMS Berwick* was a type 12M (modified) Rothesay Class Frigate. Built by Harland & Wolff in Belfast she was commissioned in 1961. She was sunk used as target practice in 1985.
2. *HMS Lowestoft* was also a Type 12M Rothesay Class Frigate built by Stephen and Glass Sons Ltd in Glasgow. She was commissioned in 1961 and sunk as a target in exercises during 1986.

Chapter 15

CAPTAIN FISH

In 1977 I was promoted to Captain and appointed to the challenging dual jobs of Captain Fishery Protection and Captain Mine Counter Measures.

Britain had just declared an Exclusive Fishery Zone of 200 miles. My job was to protect our waters from any foreign fisherman catching our fish; and ensure the effectiveness of the mine counter-measures in place, to enable the UK to keep its ports open and their approaches clear of mines in a time of conflict with anyone.

In all I had 32 ships under my overall command. We were not at war, but we did need to control the overfishing of our waters by foreign fishing fleets.

My base was in Rosyth, Scotland and I worked very closely with the Ministry of Agriculture and Fisheries. As we did not have enough specialist ships, I was given a frigate to help control our territorial waters. I could in an emergency call on Nimrods (planes) as well.

Jersey Fishery Protection, oil rig protection.

Oil rig protection.

I was responsible for introducing a new class of Fishery Protection vessels (the Island Class) which would also patrol our oil rigs. *HMS Jersey* was the first of her class, followed by five others. They were fast and sufficiently armed and were a useful addition to the protection fleet.

The first incursion into our new territorial waters was a Russian fishing ship.

She was intercepted and taken to the Shetlands, to appear in front of the local Sheriff. Up till now, fishing infringements had been dealt with by local magistrates and fines were a few thousand pounds. The Sheriff had greater powers and fined the Russian £50,000. We were thrilled. At last we seemed to be getting civilian back up, with suitable financial deterrents. We also confiscated his nets. Getting his nets off on to the jetty was a stupendous job and we wondered what to do with them, so we decided that, in future, the cost of dealing with the confiscated nets would be added to the fine. In this case, he bought his nets back from us. It had been an expensive trip for him.

* * * * *

The channel is divided on the French and British side by a series of lines difficult to identify at sea. It can be complicated to know whether you are in French or British waters. We had established an operation in the Channel and one day I was awoken by the Duty Officer who told me he had one of my Commanding Officers on the line from his ship, who wanted to speak me.

He told me he'd just stopped and sent a boarding party on to a French fishing vessel clearly in British waters. The boarding party consisted of three unarmed men, whose job was to inspect the net size and the size of the catch. This group might include the cook, or someone like that, but all the people in a boarding party of the British protection fleet were multi trained. Having got this party on board, the French Captain had taken off at full speed and was heading for French waters with our men still in situ.

He added they were still chasing the fishing vessel and were all still in British waters. He asked me what my orders were and I told him to carry on and keep in close contact. I then rang the MoD for instructions. We ended up with me, my advisor and representatives from the MoD, the Ministry of Agriculture of Fisheries and the Foreign Office, in a five-way conversation with the Captain of the chasing ship. Eventually we got a message which said 'I'm right over his stern. Shall I drop my anchor, Sir?' The temptation to say, 'Aye!' to this was enormous, but it would probably have caused an international incident if we'd sunk a French fishing vessel on purpose. Instead we authorised him to put a shot across the bow of the French vessel, which had no effect whatsoever. The French fishing party just carried on to Le Havre.

Docking in the port, they had a welcome party of French police, and the crew were arrested and interrogated. Our captured boarding party were taken discreetly by the French gendarmerie to Calais for a return trip to Dover. In case the press got word of this little incident, we decided to remove our captured boarding party from the ferry before it docked, and sent a Royal Marine fast boat to pick them up from the ferry, which had stopped a mile short of Dover to allow the transfer. They were reunited with their ship a few hours later.

* * * * *

In my role as Captain of Fishery Protection and Mine Counter-Measures I had a large number of minesweepers under my command. One particular minesweeper had been off the Berwick Tweed area, where they were policing the waters and trying to stop the salmon being poached by boats from both local and foreign fishing fleets. One fishing boat saw the patrol boat approaching and beat it as fast as possible into a little harbour, one too shallow for us to follow him. What he did not know was that we had a helicopter on patrol, too. The helicopter followed these chaps on to the jetty where they ran ashore into a house. A little later they came out the back of the house carrying a rolled up carpet gently between them. It was of course full of freshly caught salmon. We called up the local police who intercepted them and confiscated the salmon. The salmon would end up in our freezer stores, as possible evidence. We were usually supplied with lovely fresh fish caught legally by British fishing vessels.

When I was up at Rosyth, I was tasked by the Ministry to lead a delegation to Malta in order to talk to Mr Mintoff, the Prime Minister, about some of the military paraphernalia that was left behind when we withdrew from Malta, on her independence. This included barges.

My team, including people from the MoD and Foreign Office flew out to Malta, where the High Commissioner met us. The diplomats were in a great state of worry, as they thought Mr Mintoff might use our negotiations to negotiate some other points of discussion. So, thoroughly briefed, we went to our meeting. The other side was led by a senior civil servant in Malta who was an extremely nice man and we both got on very well together.

The negotiations were tough, we didn't yield much and they didn't yield much, but we came to a satisfactory conclusion about which barges would be returned to the UK and which would stay on the island.

At about 4pm, on the second day, we had finished our dealings and the Maltese team told us that they now would have to report to Mr Mintoff and let him know what we had agreed.

We all duly filed through into a suitably impressive suite of rooms and Mr Mintoff entered and welcomed us. He suggested we report on our proceedings first, followed by the Maltese senior civil servant.

After hearing both sides, Mr Mintoff exploded with rage. We suffered a few minutes of this rant then he calmed himself down and finally accepted our agreement. He had made his point and reminded us who was boss. That night, our last, we were going to a nice restaurant in the south eastern tip of the island.

As we were walking across the square to our cars, one of Mr Mintoff's aides ran out and said breathlessly, 'Captain Dingemans, Mr Mintoff wants to see you.' I thought we'd blown it after all. So I said to the other chaps, 'I'll meet you at the restaurant when I've finished and let you know what's going on.'

With that, they went off for dinner and I returned to Mr Mintoff's office again. He greeted me with a handshake and told me how much he had enjoyed our visit. He had however forgotten one thing. He said he had meant to give me a gift. With a flourish he produced from his pocket, a lovely green book, filled with First Issue stamps celebrating Malta's independence, something I still treasure.

Mr Mintoff then said he knew I was going to this particular restaurant and I was going to be late. He offered to provide a car for me, so I could join the others who were now sitting in the restaurant wondering whether the two rather strenuous days negotiating had been a waste of time.

Looking out the window they saw a very smart Rolls-Royce pull up. While they were wondering who the VIP was, out I popped, having been lent Mr Mintoff's private car for the evening. A generous gesture and much appreciated.

A year later, another Captain was appointed to the Mine Counter-Measures task, as my time had become totally occupied with Fishery Protection.

Chapter 16

RCDS

On completion of my tour of duty in Fishery Protection, in 1979 I joined the one year course at the Royal College of Defence Studies; this brings together senior officers from combined forces, from all over the world, in the hope that they will forge lasting friendships and at the very least, learn to respect each other. Our group consisted of 50 British and 39 foreign students. Most of us became Admirals, Generals and Air Marshalls and leaders. It gave us all great contacts worldwide.

In the third term of the course, the students go on a tour of different overseas countries. There are about five separate tours, but ours took in Germany, France, Turkey and Cyprus.

Each group would visit their chosen locations and were received by the top brass and management of each country; the idea being that each group would also form lasting friendships with colleagues in these countries. We arrived in Hamburg where we were met by a consul who said he was afraid there had been a mix up with the hotel bookings and we would be not be staying in hotel X but would have similar accommodation in Hotel Y. So we reloaded our bags on to the transport provided and went to Hotel Y.

We were a mixed bunch of nationalities, about 16 in all and split into pairs, we were to share eight bedrooms. Keys were handed to each pair and the manager escorted us up to a long corridor, where we were staying. There was a mass exodus of the corridor and a mass shutting of doors as we all went into our rooms. Within four seconds, all the doors opened again and the corridor was full of complaining voices.

The booking clerk had misunderstood. Instead of twin beds each 'couple' had been given a double bed. We were not having any of that. We could imagine the newspaper headlines and, as our Israeli colleague pointed out, if anyone heard he was sharing a bedroom, let alone a bed, with an Arab, there would be uproar. Twin beds were found for all.

*   *   *   *   *

Part of the training was a visit to the British Army Base in Cyprus. Our hosts asked us to a barbeque lunch on the beach on the Sunday. We set off, and as we walked down a little slipway to the gathering on the beach I looked up and there, on either side of this slipway, were a large number of Royal Marines, clearly off duty and clearly enjoying themselves.

I went and saw the Sergeant Major and warned him that there could be some trouble between the forces if the jollity and drinking went too far. Not everyone of our party understood British Forces sense of humour. We sat down on this lovely beach and were wined and dined like royalty. No tartan rugs and wasps for us. The serried ranks of tables were covered with crisp white cloths, laid with the best silver cutlery and the glistening crystal glasses were filled with delicious Cypriot wine. And bless those Royal Marines, they were as good as gold, but they couldn't resist giving a little cheer, as we sat down to enjoy our sumptuous feast.

The RCDS Mission Statement is:

"To prepare senior officers and officials of the United Kingdom and other countries and future leaders from the private and public sectors for high responsibilities in their respective organizations, by developing their analytical powers, knowledge of defence and international security, and strategic vision."

At the end of this course we were expected to write a paper with one of our fellow students. My colleague and I wrote a paper entitled: RECOMMENDATIONS TO THE CHIEFS OF STAFF. In this book I include a small extract for the reader to ponder. Ask yourself, if these recommendations have stood the test of time. For the record these recommendations were written in 1979.

"SUMMARY OF CONCLUSIONS AND RECOMMENDATIONS

The evolution of the role of the Chiefs of Staff has been generally responsive to change in world and national affairs, and no fundamental changes are advocated.

The Chiefs of Staff should exercise a more demonstrative role within their own services.

In the wider realms of national leadership there has been diminishing respect and confidence. This trend should be reversed, and leaders should become better known to the general public. They should expound their views and exhibit their qualities instead of reacting to the initiative of the less powerful and intelligent. The Chiefs of Staff should play their part by keeping the nation informed of government policy on defence.

There exists no channel for the public representation of the views of servicemen on conditions of service despite the burgeoning of unions and other groups in our society.

It is believed that a safety valve is required and that examination should be made of the procedures for the Defence Select Committee of the House of Commons with a view of granting constitutional dispensation to the Chiefs of Staff to make representations under certain circumstances.

The Chiefs of Staff have a leading role to play in the formulation of NATO strategy (in the aftermath of the Salt II agreement) as a bridge between the United States and Europe.

In the operational field the role of the Chiefs of Staff in the control of national operations and the arrangement for the preparation of forces assigned to NATO work well. Their role in minor operations, particularly those of a peacekeeping nature, must ensure that the commander in the field is not placed in an invidious military position in the furtherance of political aims. They must further ensure that the power of the media is understood and that their advice to the Government reflects this understanding.

The Chiefs of Staff involvement in equipment matters has increased over the years, and will not diminish, rather will they be faced with many difficult and potentially divisive decisions during the 1980s. They should be united in their advice to Ministers eschewing fratricidal strife whilst seeking equipment which are both flexible in their use and permit improvement during their life.

The Chiefs of Staff should press for political initiatives in the European defence industry to standardization of equipments and improvement in efficiency of procurement."

After finishing the RCDS course my next appointment was to command *HMS Intrepid.*

END OF PART ONE

PART 2

INTREPID

Chapter 17

HMS INTREPID

My appointment to *HMS Intrepid*[1], first time round, was in 1980. I was thrilled, having just finished the Royal College of Defence Studies (RCDS) course, which is widely recognised as the elite course for future leaders in public service. Those on the course were expected to achieve Flag rank or the equivalent in other forces or the civil service.

A Landing Platform Dock's (LPD) or Assault ship's role was to provide support to the Royal Marines amphibious assault force and to support the army should they need to use amphibious landing craft.

The ship is virtually a streamlined floating dock with a 3 storey stowage space for vehicles surrounded by accommodation for the ship's company and military personnel, and surmounted by a flight deck. She carried in her dock four large landing craft (LCU) and four small sized landing craft (LCVP) at davits (small cranes for suspending and lowering boats), from which she could land forces from

Intrepid.

Intrepid *arriving in Sweden.*

sea to a location of her choice. Her ship's company numbered about 500. She could carry up to 2000 people on board, although that could get a little crowded.

She had the capability to carry six 30-ton tanks, three helicopters and multi-purpose stores and other logistics. During amphibious operation the ship becomes a joint headquarters for naval and military commanders.

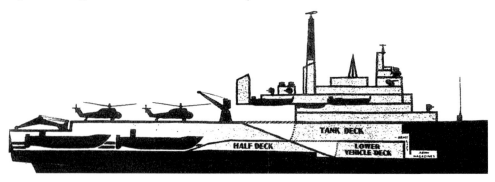

Intrepid, *showing vehicle deck.*

Intrepid, *showing dock.*

Army exercising with Royal Navy.

Chieftain Tank coming ashore from Intrepid.

Intrepid *(stern view).*

She carried four Seacat missiles systems and two 40mm Bofor guns for defence against surface or air attack.

When not used for amphibious duties *HMS Intrepid* was used as a Dartmouth training ship and, as such, went to the Mediterranean in the autumn, The West Indies in the spring, and the Baltic in the summer with about 150 midshipmen on board. The object was to teach these young sailors what it was like to be at sea and to visit a large number of foreign ports, both to broaden their education and Fly the Flag.

We would take the 150 midshipmen in three separate groups away in her for about three months at a time and they would learn the art of being at sea, from navigation to lowering and handling landing craft, from swimming off the stern gates to piping the Admiral on board. It may sound a bit old fashioned but it taught the midshipmen the codes of conduct and professionalism expected from them as members of the Royal Navy. More importantly, it gave them a real taste of what life at sea was all about.

On this particular occasion we were going to visit Greece during the Mediterranean tour. We arrived off Piraeus, the port for Athens. It was a lovely calm day so we were relaxed while we waited for the pilot to come out and take us in.

Naval ships are not dependent on the pilot, but sensibly would take a pilot on board when going into a narrow harbour, which is what we were planning to do.

We eventually saw the small pilot ship leaving the shore and heading our way. The launch moored up under the ladder and the pilot and his assistant stepped on to the bridge saying portentiously: 'Sir, you are the luckiest Captain in the whole world. I am the best pilot in all Greece.' We all smiled at each other, shook hands and made ready to enter the harbour.

Intrepid *in the West Indies.*

Hands to bathe.

I had worked out carefully with the navigator where we were going to drop two anchors as, in the Mediterranean, rather than go along side, you drop anchors and back on to the jetty. This enables more ships to be put in, but it can be a problem when you try and pick the anchors up again.

We headed off and were soon through the harbour entrance successfully and very shortly after we should have been dropping the first anchor. Unfortunately, at this very moment, an argument broke out between the senior pilot and his assistant. They were gesticulating madly at each other and towards the shore. They were steadily building their dispute into a full scale war; their voices were rising by the minute and feet were beginning to stamp.

It was obvious to me and the rest of the crew on the Bridge, that this argument was going to take precedence over dropping anchors, so the navigator gave me the nod when the first anchor needed to be dropped. I passed the order down and the anchor rattled out. We then ran on and dropped the second anchor and started to back on to the jetty.

This manoeuvre went on for some time, as the space between both anchors was very narrow and so involved a fair amount of forward and reverse movements. Our

Intrepid *stern board in Naples.*

pilots meanwhile were oblivious, still gesticulating in the background, their personal vendetta far outweighing the minor problems we were encountering.

Eventually we berthed alongside, just in time for the British Ambassador and his party of VIPs to arrive. The Royal Marine band played and a great time was had by all. The two pilots decamped bowing and glowing with self congratulations, with the certain knowledge of a job well done!

The next stop was Egypt. We stopped outside the port of Alexandria and waited for the pilot boat to arrive. This it did very efficiently and the pilot came on to the Bridge. His first words were: 'Sir, you are the luckiest Captain in the world, as I am the finest pilot in all Egypt.' The Bridge could hardly stifle our laughter. One of the snags in a ship like *Intrepid* is the very high bow. If you are not careful the wind will take the bow away from the jetty just when you think you're secure. Modern ships would have a bow thruster which simplifies things considerably. In our case, as there was a wind blowing off the jetty, I told the pilot I'd like a tug to hold up my bow. His reaction was a little startling. He said, with real passion, that he would not employ them.

'Why not? They're yours,' I said.

'I would not trust them,' was his doom laden reply. I persisted and he said with resignation, 'If you want a tug, Captain, you will have one.' The tug, summoned from its anchorage, rushed across and smashed straight into my bow! The pilot turned to me and said sadly, 'I told you so, Captain.'

*　　*　　*　　*　　*

The American Navy, ahead of us all, had taken women on board as part of their ship's company. The first woman at sea was on a US support ship, which was taking part in a NATO amphibious exercise in northern Norway.

The British Admiral was flying his Flag on *Intrepid* and he and I went off in a helicopter to look at some beaches which might be suitable for the joint exercise landings. We said we'd be back at 12pm. In fact, with the adverse weather conditions prevailing, we completed our beach survey sooner than expected and arrived back at the ship at 11.30am, ready to touch down. The flight deck was not manned and the ship seemed deserted. The Admiral was still on the helicopter so we flew round and round the ship with the co-pilot sticking his hand out the window patting his arm trying to indicate to the one individual who had wandered out on to the deck that there was gold braid on board. When we finally caught his attention the flight deck rapidly went into top gear and we touched down. The Admiral was unimpressed by this reception and even less impressed when he discovered why *Intrepid's* hospitality and readiness was below par.

In our absence, 12 American female sailors had been invited to tour the ship and have a welcome drink afterwards. The ship's company was falling over themselves to show them around their part of the ship and, as a consequence, failed to notice our return. The guests were sent packing by the Admiral, who was angry that the ship had had no lookout on deck.

*　　*　　*　　*　　*

The Norwegian fjords were a magnificent sight both by day and by night, but anchoring was very difficult because of the depth of water, which required us to put all our anchor cable out.

When we came to weigh later on we immediately hit problems. Our capstan (a rotating drum around which cable is wound, used for heavy weights like anchor cable) struggled with its task and blew all the fuses guarding the motors and I thought we would be there for the duration unless we managed to get the anchor cable up.

The second and the third attempts failed and I envisaged a dark scenario, where I would have to break the cable and then request for it to be recovered at some later date by a specialist group. The fourth time luck was on our side and we hauled it in very, very slowly.

*   *   *   *   *

In our role as Dartmouth training ship, we visited the Virgin Islands in The West Indies. We anchored not too far off the shore of a beautiful beach. Most of the ship's company and 150 cadets were shuttled to shore by a series of landing craft and we had a wonderful barbeque picnic and a very pleasant day of sports and swimming competitions on the magnificent beach.

For many of these cadets this was their first experience of the wonderful Caribbean lifestyle and they certainly seemed enthusiastic. Just before night fall, we had to get moving. When lowering the stern gate on *Intrepid*[2], you are restricted to four knots and you cannot go astern. We thought everything was in hand, but one of the LCU's had stuck on the sand and it took a bit of time to get it free. Meanwhile we had weighed anchor, and waiting for the LCU to dock was testing our nerve. I and the navigator on the Bridge were watching the coral shoals getting ever closer and the passage ever narrower, there being only one way through the reef. We could not change course and there was nothing we could do, until we had the LCU safely docked.

Volleyball.

Barbados and West Indies barbeque.

Those in the stranded LCU were in my mind, in danger of becoming little Robinson Crusoes, but they finally managed to free themselves and were docked. With the de-ballasting starting immediately, we raised the stern gates and were safely on our way. It was a very close thing, but yet another useful lesson on controlling the ship.

My time on *Intrepid* came to an end at the same time as the huge defence cuts introduced by Mrs Thatcher's government began to take effect. I and the ship's company left the ship which was to go into dry dock to be moth balled: we went on leave or took up our new posts.

Notes

1. *HMS Intrepid.* Intrepid was built by John Brown and Co. (Clydebank) Ltd and commissioned in March 1967. An assault ship or Landing platform Dock (LPD) her versatility was proved again and again in the Falklands conflict.

    My *Intrepid* was the 8th Royal Naval ship with that name. They were always fighting ships and I was glad that we didn't meet the fate of the 7th *Intrepid*.

The ship was at anchor off Leros, a Greek island, thinking World War 2 was over. The Captain went ashore to meet the locals, half way across three German bombers appeared from nowhere and bombed *Intrepid* which subsequently sank. The poor Captain watched helplessly as this incident occurred.

I suspect he had a similar feeling to that which I experienced when hearing a submarine has been sighted by *Intrepid* when I was at a meeting on *Fearless*.

2. How we landed the troops from the LPD was a complicated procedure, so I asked one of *Intrepid's* former engineers to explain the process. It is the best explanation I have ever read. It illustrates why later in the Falklands conflict I was worried about making myself a sitting duck during amphibious landings.

In order to launch, or 'float off', the landing craft in the rear of the ship it was first necessary to flood the dock in which the landing craft sat whilst in transit at sea. This was achieved by admitting hundreds of tons of sea water into the ship's ballast tanks, designed to ensure that the ship could rapidly sink down in order to launch the landing craft and thereafter, if necessary, pump out the ballast water and get out of harm's way if assaulting an opposed landing. The system was controlled by the hull officer of the shipwright branch with engineers manning the pumps. The latter were four very powerful steam turbine reversible 1000 tons/hours pumps two in each Engine Room, forward and aft (A and B pumps forward and X and Y pumps aft). Water was transferred round the ship via an enormous ring main which consisted mainly of a three foot wide pipe manufactured from glass resin in order to reduce both cost and weight. The procedure started with a call from Command to take the ship to 'pre-action' condition. Water was admitted to the ships ballast tanks until the ship sank down, such that the sea level was just below the large gates (the stern gate) at the back of the ship through which the landing craft would make their exit. The pumps could be used to speed the sinking down or the tanks could be allowed to free flood. All was controlled by the hull officer via a pneumatic 'computer' which sent and received air signals to the pumps and valves controllers which were, in turn, pneumatically operated.

Pre-action reduced the amount of time it took to 'go deep' to the depth needed to launch the landing craft. At the same time it allowed the ship to manoeuvre at up to 11 knots ahead and to go astern if necessary both could be vital in a combat landing zone. Once at the landing craft launch zone the order was given to go deep and the pumps would be 'clutched to ballast' and drive water into the ship's ballast tanks at full speed. At the same time, the bolts would be released and the 80-ton stern gate would open 5-degrees using hydraulic power. As the ship sank down sea water would pour in through the gap between

Divisions inspected by the Captain.

the stern gate and the ship, flooding the dock and greatly speeding the sinking process. Once at action depth, the landing craft could embark men, vehicles or tanks. The gate was then carefully fully lowered and the landing craft could drive out and carry out their tasks. The ship itself could still drive forward if required but only at four knots. Astern movement was unadvisable since it could cause a mini tidal wave to race up the armoured beach and into the vehicle deck. Once the operation was completed, landing craft could be re-embarked; a potentially hazardous operation as the craft could bounce violently in even a moderate seaway, making for dangerous conditions for those handling the ropes of the craft and in the small catwalk around the dock. The gate would then be raised to 5-degrees and the four pumps would be clutched to de-ballast and, with a roar like Concorde taking off, thrust hundreds of tons of water from the ballast tanks and back into the sea. As the ship consequently rose in the water, the sea water in the dock would now start to pour out of the 5-degree gap. Eventually the gate would be fully closed, residual sea water drained from the dock via scuppers and eight bolts inserted each side of the gate to ensure it could not inadvertently open. All of this was carried out smartly since the ship may well be trying to exit the aforementioned combat zone, 45 minutes being the desired time for de-ballasting.

Chapter 18

THE FALKLANDS ISLANDS CONFLICT

Falklands Conflict

On 2 April 1982 Argentine forces invaded the Falkland Islands. Britain assembled, trained and launched a naval task force to sail 8,000 miles to retake the islands. 74 days later on 14 June 1982 Argentine Forces surrendered. The cost in lives was 258 British sailors, marines, Royal Fleet Auxiliary, Merchant Navy, soldiers, airmen and Falkland Islanders; and 649 Argentine army, navy, marines, airmen, border guard, coastguard and civilian sailors; plus ships, helicopters and aircraft on both sides.

On 3 April 1982 Argentine forces invaded South Georgia. Britain sent a small naval task group to retake the island and 13 days later on Argentine forces surrendered, giving rise to the legendary signal from the landing force commander, Major Guy Sheridan, Royal Marines: 'Be pleased to inform Her Majesty that the White Ensign flies alongside the Union Jack in South Georgia. God save the Queen.' The cost in lives was three Argentine marines during their invasion and one Argentine sailor in a tragic incident during the operation to recapture the island.

*   *   *   *   *

I include an extract from the book *Signals of War The Falklands Conflict of 1982* written by Virginia Gamba-Stonehouse and the historian Sir Lawrence Freedman, Vice Principal Strategy & Development and Professor of War Studies, King's College London. I personally find that it offers the clearest view of the history of the Falklands I have ever read.

"In the 16th Century Britain, Spain and Portugal all laid claim to the Falkland Islands.

In 1765 Port Egmont was established as a British settlement and Sovereignty was claimed for King George III in 1766. This led to disputes with Spain who were also present on the Islands, which nearly led to war.

In 1770 a treaty settled the matter and both countries continued to reside.

In 1771 the British returned for a few years.

In 1774 Britain withdrew from several settlements across the world, including the Falklands. Importantly they left a plaque claiming sovereignty on the Falklands.

Spain withdrew in 1806 leaving a plaque making a similar claim.

The first Argentine flag was raised on the Falkland Islands on the 6 November 1820 by the new Government of the United Provinces of the Rio de la Plata as part of its effort to establish its right to the former possessions of Spain.

In 1829 a Frenchman Louis Vernet was appointed Governor and played a leading role in attempting to establish a settlement on the island, interestingly enough this episode mirrored the dispute between the British and the Argentines, but in this case it was the Americans. Vernet sought to enforce Argentine fishing rights by seizing three American fishing ships which were claimed by the US Government to be engaged in a lawful trade. In response the USS Lexington sailed to the Island, landed, destroyed all military installations, raised the buildings putting most of the inhabitants under arrest and the left, declaring the Island free of all government.

On the 10 September 1832 Buenos Aires appointed an interim Military & Political commander and dispatched a gunboat called the *ARA Sarandi* to do repairs and restore order. However, two months later whilst the gunboat was away from the island the garrison revolted killing the new Governor. The *Sarandi* returned and attempted to rout the Mutineers.

In all this the British still had their claim to sovereignty too. So it was understandable that the British warship *HMS Clio* was sent by the British Admiralty to reassert the British claim. When she appeared in Puerto Soledad, the Captain of *Clio* told the Captain of the *Saranandi* that the British Flag would replace the Argentine Flag on the 3 of January 1833. Due to the superior fire power of the British the Captain of the *Sarandi* protested but with no shots fired departed taking the Argentine element from the island. Duly on the 3 January 1883 the flag was lowered by the crew of a British Warship and replace by a British flag.

(It was not lowered again for 149 years when the Argentine forces occupied the islands. British forces lowered the Argentine flag on the 14 June 1982.)

The islands were formally established as Crown Colony in 1840, the first Governor arriving in 1841.

2 April – 6 May 1982: UK to Ascension Island

On 2 April 1982 my last Command *HMS Intrepid* was sitting in a dry dock awaiting either sale to a foreign navy or a refit and on that same day Rex Hunt, the Governor of the Falkland Islands, surrendered to the invading Argentines who, with a force of 900, easily overcame the 68 British Royal Marines stationed in the Falkland capital, Port Stanley.

The Thatcher Government was in the process of cutting the defence budget radically and had been taking a hefty pruning knife to all the armed forces and the Royal Navy in particular (as the current coalition government is doing today in 2012).

HMS Intrepid had been one of the casualties. Another was *HMS Endurance.* The decision to retire her and close down the British Antarctic Survey at the Grytviken Base on South Georgia was to have long reaching consequences to the Falkland Islands and to *HMS Intrepid* and her former officers and crew.

During my first term as Captain of *Intrepid* (1980/1982) I and many of the ship's company had spent two and a half years travelling the globe.

A Landing Platform Dock (LPD) is an amphibious assault ship providing support for the Royal Marines and the Army in times of war and/or periods of tension. In peacetime her role was to be the Dartmouth Training Squadron where, for three-month stints, we would take approximately 150 midshipmen to sea and teach them everything they needed to know about life at sea: from navigation to letting down and handling landing craft; from swimming off the lowered stern door to piping the Admiral on board. After many exercises, in many different harbours, waters and weather conditions, the ship's company knew both her merits and her vagaries and, boy, did she have some vagaries. There was no equipment or procedure, landing craft or engine that had not been tried and tested by the officers, midshipmen and crew who made up the ship's company. We were a tight ship and had up-to-date, specialist knowledge and a deep understanding of all phases of amphibious operations which, of course, include land operations. It had been a sad day when, in early 1982, we had left the ship to be de-commissioned and, as we thought, to be stripped out and put into mothballs.

On 5 April 1982, having left *Intrepid* I had just completed the handover in London to my new appointment, which was as Captain of the Royal Naval Presentation Team. The job of this team was to publicise the role of the Royal Navy in modern warfare and emphasize its function as a peacekeeping defence tool rather than an aggressive war tool. My role would be to make sure the Royal Navy was seen in the best light, working as a sort of Public Relations Officer. The Argentine invasion of the Falkland Islands and the British Military Task Force which, with much rattling of sabres, was rapidly being formed to retake them, was going to make my work publicising our role as peacekeepers challenging.

The formalities of the handover were completed, and we were having the hello/farewell drinks with my predecessors and my new staff, when I received an urgent phone call from the Ministry of Defence. I was to report to the Second Sea Lord.

Driven across London to the MoD at high speed, I received instructions to head to Portsmouth immediately. Once there, I was to retake command of *HMS Intrepid,* work her up as soon as possible, and join the rest of the Task Force which would be waiting for me at Ascension Island.

The navy had managed to return all but two of my original officers and 20 ratings from the original crew, who were familiar with the ship, and were being brought back from all over the world.

We were to be part of the hastily formed British Task Force, which set sail from Portsmouth to Ascension Island on 5 April 1982 in a bid to encourage the Argentines to leave the Falkland Islands.

Ascension Island was a refuelling and gathering point. It was also where we all hoped we would receive news that a diplomatic settlement had been reached.

The American Secretary of State Al Haig was practising shuttle diplomacy in his efforts to mediate between the two countries. President Reagan and most members of the EEC were putting enormous pressure on President Galtieri to find a diplomatic settlement.

A ship in Reserve resembles a filleted fish. You're left with the bare bones and a dismembered body. It was essential to have engineers who knew the engines and a ship's company which had a strong group identity. The incredible achievement of getting *Intrepid* stored, ammunition on board and fuelled for war in less than a fortnight was due to the fact that we were surrounded by familiar faces, who had trained together, run ashore together and lived socially together. Morale was high, based upon trust in one's colleagues, a cause we believed in, freedom of the individual and knowing the country was behind us.

Intrepid *leaving Portsmouth.*

Although we had to beg, borrow and steal to get the old girl up and running and fit for purpose, we were for once at the top of the list when it came to requests for parts or trained manpower to fit them.

The South Atlantic is an unforgiving sort of place and as a minimum you want to feel confident that nuts and bolts are tight and engines running smoothly. *Intrepid* was a big ship, she could be carrying up to 2000 people and essential equipment and stores, and I wanted to be sure that all would be as safe as possible.

It was an emotional departure from Portsmouth. The thousands of people lining the beachfront and every available vantage point on the harbour cheered and wept as *HMS Intrepid* steamed slowly out of the harbour. Banners, reminiscent of the departure of the main Task Force of ten or so days earlier, were waved and held aloft.

A few mornings earlier you would not have found me on the Bridge of my ship, but behind the wheel of my car. I was sitting outside Chichester Driving Test Centre, waiting to see if my son James would pass his driving test. His success had become a sort of nonsensical talisman, unspoken but deeply felt: *If James passes his test, we will get back safely from the Falklands.* James came up trumps and a few days later *Intrepid* sailed off to Ascension Island without ceremony.

We sailed from Portsmouth to Portland on 15 April for sea trials and to work-up the ship to full readiness. Just off the Isle of Wight, the Chief Engineer and I decided that we would test the brakes. We wound the ship up to 18 knots and I ordered full astern, which normally means that all restrictions on the use of equipment are off. We came to a shuddering halt and a telephone call from the engine room shattered our confidence: the condensers which produce all our fresh water had failed.

We had, the chief engineer informed me, two options: go back to Portsmouth or remain at 4 knots on a discreet night trip to our original destination, Portland in Devon. There was no choice. I wasn't going to boost Argentine morale by limping back into port. Instead, under cover of darkness and overtaken by many smaller boats, we made it into Portland for repairs. If this had happened on our way to Ascension it would have caused us terrible problems. The world and his wife seemed to descend on the ship once we arrived and in a short time we were ready to resume our sea trials and work up.

At Portland we were not the only ship testing our readiness for war and it is a tribute to the Base that so much was achieved by them in so short a time. Given that the ship had regained the majority of its company I was confident that we could be operational fairly quickly. We would have time to hone everything to full readiness for war on the way south. But it was a daunting task.

HMS Intrepid had to be brought back up to full fighting efficiency as a warship. This meant testing, calibrating and exercising everything from the engine room upwards, including machinery drills, action stations, damage control, Nuclear Biological and Chemical Defence (NBCD), anti-aircraft tracking and firing the guns and Sea Cat missiles; replenishing stores and fuel at sea, boat lowering, 'man overboard' and darkening ship; and many others to name.

The ship also had to be brought back up to full fighting efficiency as an amphibious ship, specifically an LPD configured to act as a headquarters for amphibious operations. This meant testing and exercising everything from the dock upwards including ballasting, embarking and disembarking the Landing Craft Utility (LCU), lowering and recovering the Landing Craft Vehicle and Personnel (LCVP), flying stations, vectoring drills, embarked force facilities and amphibious command and control procedures, to name but a few.

On Monday 19 April we were ready for Flag Officer Sea Training (FOST) and his staff to begin crawling all over the ship inspecting, encouraging, cajoling, getting things fixed quickly and, above all, helping so that on Friday of that week by coincidence the anniversary of the raid on Zeebrugge by the Royal Marines in 1918 we received FOST's seal of approval and went alongside in Portland docks to complete our preparations.

Minesweeping gear laid out.

Landing craft preparing to go minesweeping. The boxes are solid magnets.

As we approached the harbour entrance there was a small LCVP, not belonging to us, towing something that was causing a drag wave in the water, which meant it was heavy. I thought it might be some kind of minesweeping equipment, but didn't think too much about it until two days later it arrived on board *Intrepid*.

This rather peculiar device consisted of a variety of equipment, including a noise generator and enormous, permanent magnets encased in a wooden box. This was our minesweeper. When towed behind a small LCVP, driven by two very brave coxswains, this Heath Robinson contraption would, we were assured, clear any enemy mines for the passage of all our ships and troop movements. For the duration of our voyage the huge magnets were stored on the tank deck, giving rise to some curious local anomalies, but we were to use them later.

*   *   *   *   *

Our promised week was up. Soon after we berthed that Friday we were ordered to sail on the Monday. Our final preparations had shrunk to two days. The powers that be were very determined that we should join the rest of the Task Force at Ascension Island as rapidly as possible.

Those two days were full of frantic activity. Our embarked force arrived, a far more diverse group than the landing force that we had grown accustomed to. The bulk comprised 128 officers and men from the Commando Logistic Regiment, Royal Marines, led by the Regiment's second-in-command. Determined not to be left behind, he had formed this group of logisticians into a composite rifle company and convinced the powers that be that he should take them south. There was a detachment of 28 officers and men from 845 Naval Air Squadron together with two Wessex helicopters, a ferry and maintenance crew of eight, with a replacement Sea King Mk 4, the last in the UK, for one that had been lost a week earlier; a small party from 12 Air Defence Regiment Royal Artillery to augment technical support for the Rapier Air Defence Battery, already embarked in the main force; and five Communications and Electronic Warfare specialists, who were to prove invaluable in giving us early warning of air raids from Argentina. All their equipment came too, including two bulldozers, a miscellany of mobile radios, the aforementioned magnets and minesweeping equipment and the necessary logistics of war.

At the same time, more general stores were embarked to stretch food endurance to a maximum. As all the storerooms were full, a false floor of boxes of tinned goods had to be created throughout the main passageways, which meant we were bent over while walking along corridors, creating some unusual walking styles reminiscent of the Ministry of Silly Walks.

Little did we realize that over the next five weeks we would play host to 4,750 'visitors'. We were to have on board the Commandos and Paras, the Scots Guards, the SAS and the Gunners. We would be used for the reception of casualties, prisoners, fire fighters and Special Forces. We ferried troops, went mine hunting and acted as an Exocet decoy. We repaired ships, washed laundry and operated helicopters and landing craft throughout the war.

But for now it was time to say our goodbyes and, despite the pressure of that weekend, we granted leave to those of the ship's company who could be spared. Then, in one of those curiously Royal Naval moments, the civilian Chinese laundrymen disembarked on Sunday, at which point we knew that diplomacy wasn't working and we would probably have to fight to retake the Falklands.

*　　*　　*　　*　　*

On Monday 26 April, just three weeks after the main task force had left, we faced the day of our departure from Portland. Once clear of the breakwater, we ballasted deep (filled the chamber with water), lowered the stern door and embarked the landing craft. A little after midday we embarked the Sea King and two Wessex helicopters and, with those last items loaded, we set sail for Ascension Island.

As we steamed south, we heard the welcome news that South Georgia had been retaken. The Task Force had lost two Wessex helicopters that crashed in atrocious weather and the Argentines lost one Petty Officer, killed in a tragic misunderstanding after they had surrendered one submarine.

On board *Intrepid* the hard work continued, bringing all the officers and crew up to speed with equipment and procedures. We had to ensure that we were ready for any role thrown at us and that everyone on board operated as an efficient team. For the next nine days there was endless training and practice at every conceivable drill: action stations, defence stations, 'abandon ship' drills, damage control drills, at all times of day and night. By the time we arrived at Ascension we were, I believed ready for war. I have always believed that war is won by the nations and commanders who most determinedly prepare for it in peace. This does not appear to be a view influencing Government thinking.

My beliefs were mirrored on the ship we escorted south, the North Sea ferry *MV Norland* which had on board 900 paratroopers of 2nd Battalion the Parachute

Car Ferry Norland *with 2 Para embarked.*

Regiment (2 Para). Their CO, Lt Col H Jones, was embarked in *Intrepid* to take advantage of the better communications. He found the separation from his men strange and very frustrating, but he was able to get across to *Norland* regularly. They drilled and trained constantly, including a three-day amphibious acquaint courtesy of our amphibious operations team who helicoptered across each day. Their readiness for war was obvious. When you saw the distances they yomped and the weight they carried on their backs, it was clear that not much would deter these fighting men.

While sailing to Ascension we honed our existing communication systems so that we kept the whole ship informed - from the Bridge to the engine rooms, from the laundry to the gun crews. People can cope with many terrible things if they know what dangers they face and can trust those commanding the ship to keep them up to speed.

On 2 May the sinking of *ARA General Belgrano* was reported, which gave us all a tremendous boost in confidence. It was almost a false sense of security as, two days later, we received the report of the loss of *HMS Sheffield,* one of our newest ships, a Type 42 destroyer, which was hit by an Exocet missile amidships and sank. This stunned the whole ship's company, me included, and brought home to everyone in Britain and in the Task Force that we were in a shooting war.

My message to the crew was that it was up to us to ensure a successful end to the campaign, so that *Sheffield*'s loss was not in vain. The most significant strategic outcome of the *Belgrano* sinking was the elimination of the Argentine naval threat.

Exocet about to hit a Ship.

Impact.

With the exception of one conventional submarine, the whole Argentine fleet returned to port and didn't put to sea again for the duration of the conflict. Crucially, the Argentine carrier battle group withdrew, removing the direct threat to the British Task Force and forcing the Argentines to mount air attacks from the mainland virtually at the limit of their range. For the present, though, we still hoped for a diplomatic solution.

We finally joined the main amphibious Task Force at Ascension at 18.00 on 5 May. The next three days were filled with a seemingly endless arrival of helicopter transfers of stores and equipment from Wideawake, the airfield on the island, and the departure of similar loads from *Intrepid* to other ships in company. There was method in this apparent madness, as some of the stores and equipment that had been loaded so quickly in the UK to enable the Task Force to get underway needed to be redistributed to ensure that ships had what they required for their role. Our two Wessex transferred to *RFA Tidespring*, back from the successful South Georgia operation, to replace the two that had been lost and we embarked two more that had been flown out from UK as battle replacements. These were struck down (tethered) on to the tank deck to keep the flight deck free for operating the larger Sea Kings. The Rapier detachment rejoined their parent organization, and we embarked sections of a Mexeflote, a large powered pontoon used mainly for offloading stores and men.

The opportunity was also taken for more training. The LCVP minesweepers went off to work up their drills and procedures; the Logistic Regiment rifle company went ashore to train and fill sandbags; our own Internal Security Platoon continued its work-up; and the LCUs spent a lot of time with *MV Norland* on amphibious drills with 2 Para. I flew across to *Fearless* with my Amphibious Operations Officer for lengthy planning meetings.

7–20 May: Ascension Island to the Falklands

The Task Force sailed at 22.30 on 7 May and *Intrepid* remained behind to pick up any further loads due into Ascension overnight. Among other things, the loads included 14 one-ton loads of water-making equipment, destined for the cruise ship *SS Uganda* which had been commandeered and converted into a hospital ship. Cruise ships usually pick up water in port; unlike most RN ships they do not have the facilities to make their own water.

The very last cargo that we loaded was 200 boxes of tomatoes. Little did we realise that one of the store ships, which had already gone ahead, carried another 200 boxes of tomatoes, with our name on it. It is difficult for the average man to have any concept of how many that actually represents in breakfasts, lunches and dinners. Suffice to say that at *Intrepid* reunions, the mention of tomatoes turns faces green. We generously offered these tomatoes to every ship in the fleet but there were no takers. 'It must have been one zero too many, Sir!' the Stores Officer, who hadn't even requisitioned them, said, eyes rolling skyward when questioned.

* * * * *

To operate a task force at a distance of 8000 miles from base needed a huge logistic train. This was provided by the Royal Fleet Auxiliary (RFA) and about 50 merchant ships. These ships were requisitioned or chartered and were known as Ships Taken Up from Trade (STUFT). The need for this huge support force of ships, boats and tankers added a new dimension to the operation.

The support force was used as required and methods of transfer varied depending on the ships but wires, lines, helicopters and hoses all came into play.

From the very beginning of the operation, as the Task Force sailed from the UK, and Admiral Sandy Woodward's Task Group had sailed south from Gibraltar, both naval and RFA ships operated alongside each other during the whole campaign. The Task Force and the Task Group joined up sailing south to Ascension. None of the RN actions would have been possible without the untiring support of men and ships of the RFA, which were mainly crewed by civilian volunteers.

Most impressive of the lot were the fuel tankers. These crews worked 24 hours a day, as there was nowhere else to refuel other than at sea. You would be called to refuel and for four hours you would dance a tango at sea as the fuel lines connected you like all embracing limbs. Any sign or signal that enemy planes could be in the

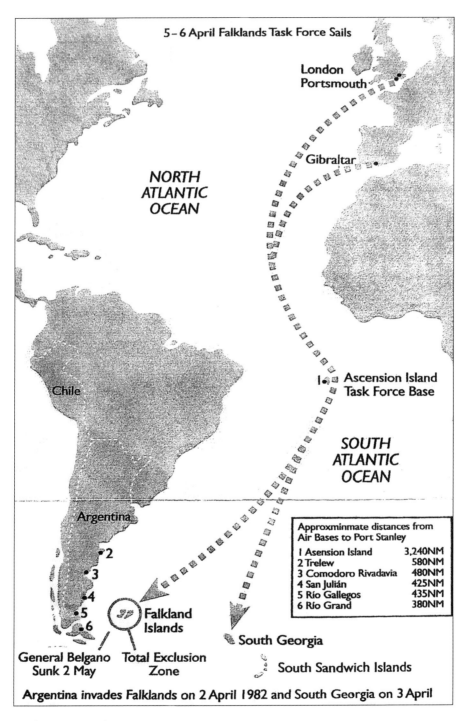

Task Force Track.

area meant a fast uncoupling. The world record of two ships refuelling just 120 feet apart is 52 hours 40 minutes. That I can assure you is an incredible achievement.

* * * * *

We were about 200 miles from the Falklands on 11 May when, because of my previous experience in anti submarine warfare, particularly on the frigates *Lowestoft* and *Berwick*, I became a little anxious about our defences against submarine attack. The Naval Captain of *Canberra,* the cruise ship which had been commandeered as a troop carrier, was also worried about his ship's vulnerability. We sent a message to Commodore Clapp expressing our concerns. He in turn called us to his ship, which was ten to 15 miles away. He was based in *HMS Fearless* my sister ship. This made it both the senior ship and the Flag ship.

Arriving by helicopter across a choppy sea we were greeted with a stern message: 'You two and the Captain of *Fearless* are to lock yourselves away in a cabin, and let me know when you are in agreement – don't bother me until you are in agreement!'

The Captain, a former submariner, produced the silver (coffee pot) and we started our deliberations over our first cup of coffee. Our host assured us both that he could guarantee that there were no submarines within 200 miles.

At that moment a message came from the Bridge: '*Intrepid* reports a periscope!' General consternation ensued. I was rushed up to the bow of the ship to await a helicopter. As I jumped from foot to foot waiting for my ride, I imagined my torpedoed ship slowly sinking into the waves.

Back on my still buoyant ship I raced to the Bridge. The leading mechanic, who had reported the sighting, described perfectly the submarine periscope.

At the time I thought that, as the whole fleet was silent, shut down with radars off, the submarine's Captain had steamed passed us as he was receiving no signals of our presence. We thought that he must have been trailing us, and unable to get a sonar fix on us, he had put up his mast hoping to sight us visually but that our luck had held out. It was the first really frightening moment I experienced. We found out later that other allied submarines had joined *HMS Conqueror* in the blockade of the Argentine coast and to report incoming air raids, so it was probably one of them, but that was later.

All the way south, planning for the landing continued apace. Having settled upon an outline plan, one of the consequential actions was to re-configure and transfer the landing force tactically into the most capable shipping force to ensure a successful amphibious assault against whatever opposition the Argentines could muster. This involved a lot of movement known as 'cross decking'. To achieve this, the first cross decking occurred on 13 May when we embarked 140 officers and men from Z Company of 45 Commando Group, Royal Marines by helicopter from *RFA Stromness.*

On 14 May we heard that Special Forces had raided Pebble Island where the Argentine navy had taken a grass strip for Pucara light ground attack aircraft and T-34 Mentors; and destroyed the lot. On 15 May I took my planning team across to *Fearless* for the Commanding Officers' briefing of the assault plan.

On 18 May I was ordered to detach and take the water distilling plant to *SS Uganda* the commandeered cruise ship now acting as hospital ship. We arrived alongside and started transferring the loads by helicopter. While we were completing this task, two contacts were detected. We weren't very far from the Argentine coast and we thought they'd rumbled us. I fired reflecting chaff rockets and drove round and round *Uganda* so as not to be a sitting duck. I only had a Bofors gun and Sea Cat missiles to defend the ship, but I was determined we were not to be a pushover.

We waited to see what might emerge through the clouds and with great relief we saw two Harriers emerge in the sky above us, recognizing us as friends, as we did them.

*   *   *   *   *

The next cross decking was the big one. The iconic cruise ship *Canberra,* now a troop carrier, retained her white livery and became known affectionately as the *Great White Whale*. We felt that it was highly likely that she would become a target. As she was carrying the Commandos and Paras who were our main fighting force, it was important they were kept safe.

On 19 May it was decided to transfer 2000 marines and soldiers from *Canberra* to *Fearless* and *Intrepid* in the middle of the South Atlantic, each ship taking approx 1000 men. The sea was too rough for the Landing Craft and transferring so many by

All planes on airfield destroyed.

Put out of action by special forces.

All planes on airfield destroyed.

Sea Harriers over Uganda *the Hospital Ship.*

jackstay would take anything up to 15 hours. After quite a lot of head scratching, we had a bit of luck. The sea became as calm as it could be in the South Atlantic, so we decided to use the LCUs (landing craft).

Canberra was steaming along at about four knots with *Intrepid* steaming one side and *Fearless* the other. The marines and soldiers, loaded down with all their gear, queued at the exit doors of *Canberra*. Both ships sent landing craft up to these exits, for them to jump into. They had had very little training for this manoeuvre, although each man had had at least one practice in *Canberra*, using the gash shutes into LCUs at Ascension Island. It took a lot of courage to make that jump, especially weighted down with loaded backpacks.

We too felt very vulnerable. With our stern gates lowered we were very exposed to attack and enemy aircraft would have had a field day if we'd been spotted. A rather black sense of humour was the most valuable weapon at this stage. For example: 'President Galtieri has been given a glass bottomed boat from which to review his fleet.' This joke may seem very insensitive in current conditions but at the time we were soon to be at war and the sentiment was understandable.

Two thousand men jumped fully laden into those landing craft and were transferred to the two LPDs. There were a few bruises, but only one broken leg. One poor man fell into the water, but as he bobbed back up he was hauled into the craft, wet and cold, but safe. The stores and heavy equipment were transferred by helicopters.

The men were now on amphibious ships, crowded into any space they could find to rest and sleep. As we had created a false floor under which we stored all the extra provisions and equipment we had on board, space was barely adequate, standing tall was a euphemism, standing hunched was more factual.

Transfer of troops to Intrepid *and* Fearless.

We were, however, nearly ready for the landings. If we lost *Canberra* now, we would lose the tactical reserve, 42 Commando Royal Marines, and their back-up logistics.

It was an incredible operation, completed successfully by very well trained forces from all the services.

I now had 1900 people on board and a very strong sense of purpose filled the ship. Even though we had mixed units, they were, for that time, *Intrepid*'s ship's company and as such my responsibility.

It was at this stage I faced one of the most testing times of my life. 150 men of the SAS and SBS, plus their 50,000 lbs of war stores, were embarked onto *Intrepid* from *Hermes* and *Invincible*. From 11am to 2am the following morning, six Sea King helicopters conducted the transfer. At 22.00 I was on the Bridge when we heard the sound of a Sabre Air Distress Beacon over the distress frequency. This could only mean one thing: one of the helicopters had ditched. I experienced a truly stomach churning feeling of dread and despair when I discovered that the missing helicopter was one with 29 fully laden personnel on board. At that moment I was vividly reminded of a genuine hero of both the first and second World Wars, Field Marshal Slim's* words, describing the ultimate test of a leader: 'Suddenly,' he said, 'everybody will stop what they are doing, look at you. No one will speak, they are only looking for leadership. You will never be more alone in your life. Their courage is ebbing and you must make it flow back.'

It was at this moment that one of the qualities of leadership not often discussed was necessary, namely the ruthless single mindedness to see the task finished to the end, no matter at what personal cost to yourself. I hope I provided the calmness and the objectivity required at that moment, impossible without faith and something much greater than oneself. Had I not believed in God and his will, moments such as these would have been more difficult to get through. I gave the order to come to starboard and steer towards the position of the crash. Only nine survived and tragically 21 died in this terrible accident. Despite that setback, Special Forces operations resumed that night, this time from *Intrepid*.

On the morning of 20 May we were just north east of the Falklands. Visibility was poor and we were surrounded by all the ships of the Task Force, a pretty formidable sight. At about 15.00 a rumour, based on a report by the BBC, swept through the ships that a draft settlement had been reached. The feeling of relief at the thought they would not have to fight was plain to see, not through any lack of courage, but because no trained member of the armed services wants to spill their own or anyone else's blood unnecessarily.

Half an hour later I was handed a signal from the Commander in Chief to all Commanding Officers. Its contents were clear enough. Negotiations with the Argentines had failed. The landing would take place as planned, the next day 21 May, at 01.30.

I don't think I have had a more unpleasant duty than having to tell the ship's company and the paratroopers that we were going to have to fight in a few hours' time. Fortunately, everybody took the news calmly, put their previous elation to one side and busied themselves in their own way for what tomorrow would bring.

I ordered the Battle Ensign to be hoisted and we turned south towards the landing area.

*   *   *   *   *

In my cabin under the glass of my desk, I placed a wise maxim. I think it originated in the First World War and this is what it said: "*War is a perpetual conflict with the unexpected, so it is impossible to proscribe before, for all the circumstances that may arise. Possess in a marked degree initiative, resource, determination and a fearlessness of responsibility.*"

The sentence about responsibility was to become very relevant.

Another piece of rather sentimental writing was circulating among the ship's company at this time. No one knows who wrote it, but it certainly did the rounds of our ship.

"*A Little Girl's Prayer*
The navy has taken my daddy away,
He's gone to the Falklands, so they say.
I don't think my Daddy wanted to fight,
But it sometimes takes courage to do what is right.
We went down to Portsmouth to wave him Goodbye!
Some people cheered, I saw my mummy cry.
'God Bless them all!' said a man in the crowd,
I thought of my Daddy and felt very proud.
The house seems so quiet since Dad went away,
Mum listens to news on the TV all day.
I hope he's safe and the seas aren't too rough,
I know I'd be scared, but I know my Dad's tough.
In church and at school we all pray for peace,
And ask that the fighting may well soon cease.
I know when it does they'll send my Dad home,
So I'll try and keep smiling and not feel too sad.
The navy has taken my Daddy away,
He's gone to the Falklands so they say.
I don't think my Daddy wanted to fight
I wish I could give him a cuddle tonight."

21–26 May: The landings in San Carlos Water and build up ashore

Before we entered San Carlos Water, one of the most important decisions we made was to sort out from where Command should be exercised. Since sailing from Ascension Island I had been either on the Bridge or in the Operations Room. Time is very short in an Exocet attack.

Delegation between officers had been our peacetime practice on our former tour in *Intrepid*, this had left the individual chatting and visiting the ship's company to my Second in Command, and this approach now began to bear fruit in very different circumstances.

The main issue was where I was going to be in situations under threat. I believed that when under attack at anchor or under way, except in extreme navigational hazards, my place was in the Operations Room, the centre of all information and, more importantly, the area with probably the best communications to the rest of the ship. So we decided my Principal Warfare Officer (PWO) should be on the Gun Direction Platform as visual Gun Direction Officer and that while at anchor in San Carlos he should, after initial general approval from me, have the authority to open fire – I would only exercise a power of veto. Likewise, the other PWO who remained in the Operations Room should have the authority to open fire and fire chaff in my absence, if in his opinion, the situation warranted it. My Second in Command would remain on the Bridge keeping a visual overview of events and fighting* the ship. My Amphibious Operations Officer would stay in the Amphibious Operations Room, right next to the ship's Operations Room, which he and his team had configured as alternate amphibious headquarters in case anything happened to *Fearless*; and in which he kept an overview of the whole operation and briefed the constantly changing daily visiting personnel to the ship.

In broad terms it had been decided to land on beaches around San Carlos Water on the north western coast of East Falkland facing into Falkland Sound. Intelligence had confirmed that there were Argentine observation posts in the vicinity but no significant defences. The approaches to Stanley, on the other hand, were heavily defended and there was a force occupying the settlements of Darwin and Goose Green. The plan was to establish a secure beach head around San Carlos Water from which to mount offensive operations, and then recapture Darwin and Goose Green before advancing and retaking Port Stanley.

The amphibious task force approached the Falkland Islands from the north, heading ostensibly towards the eastern coast of East Falkland as a feint, as intelligence indicated an Argentine submarine lurking off the NE corner of East Falkland. We then turned west towards Falkland Sound. The northern end of Falkland Sound between East and West Falklands is quite narrow before it opens out and San Carlos Water becomes visible to the east.

Landing craft head for the beach.

At 01.30 on 21 May, *Fearless* was chosen to be the first ship through for the amphibious landings. Prior to our arrival a frigate had been ordered to travel the length of the Falklands Sound with the intention that, if the area had been mined, he would set them off, a dangerous assignment. The frigate had had an uneventful trip, but there was no certainty that the Falklands Sound and approaches were completely free of mines. Our senior ship *Fearless* carried the Commodore, who was in charge of all amphibious action. She led and *Intrepid* followed.

As we silently slipped along in the darkness, we were aware that Argentine observers were positioned on Fanning Head overlooking San Carlos Water to our

More of the landing forces head for the beaches of San Carlos.

left, to report any sighting of British ships or forces. These observers had to be removed for everyone's safety, so *HMS Antrim* was sent ahead with two Wessex helicopters and a heavily armed 25-strong Special Boat Services (SBS) force to deal with them. The SBS landed under covering fire from *Antrim* and called upon the Argentines to surrender, which they refused to do. Within a few minutes we saw tracer bullets firing from both sides. To my relief ours looked much larger than the enemy's.

Once the all clear was signalled, we anchored to disembark the troops. As we let down the anchor we were very conscious that we could set off an acoustic mine, so I had ordered all personnel, except those on the Bridge, to lie down on the deck a position meant to offer more protection in the event of an explosion. I can proudly say our anchor was the first to touch Falkland's mud and we encountered no mines.

The 4,000-odd men of 3 Commando Brigade were landed as follows: 40 Commando Royal Marines from *Fearless* and 2 Para from *MV Norland* over Blue Beach at San Carlos; 3 Para from *Intrepid* over Green Beach at Port San Carlos; 45 Commando Royal marines from *RFA Stromness* over Red Beach at Ajax Bay. The subsequent build up included Royal Artillery, Royal Engineers, light tanks, and the all important Rapier missiles. 42 Commando Royal Marines remained embarked in *Canberra* as tactical reserve.

Shortly before sunrise on 22 May having completed the offload we re-anchored at the head of San Carlos Water. *Fearless* and *Intrepid* were given half of San Carlos Water respectively to oversee and we wondered whether it would be better to anchor or remain underway. It was decided that with the ships at anchor we would reduce any chance of running aground or bumping into other ships. Our minds would be focused on avoidance tactics rather than on the battle. So we anchored and although this sometimes caused problems with our line of sight, worrying if you were going to hit another ship would have been a bigger headache.

Air raids began on day one and continued throughout the operation. This next section is a flavour of the ferocious onslaught at San Carlos Water, renamed Bomb Alley, during those first days and nights.

You have to look and see *Intrepid*'s and *Fearless*'s position on the map to understand why we nearly had a blue on blue incident the first day. You also have to comprehend that the savageness of the Argentine air attack encouraged some wild shooting.

Message from *HMS Fearless* to *HMS Intrepid* in San Carlos Water:

'Would you please stop firing missiles at us.'

Message from *HMS Intrepid* to *HMS Fearless:*

'We'll stop firing at you, when you stop firing at us!'

This was not live ammunition showering down on us, but the spent shells of Sea Cat missiles, which had been fired at enemy aircraft.

First attack on Fearless.

We received some warning of air attacks. We had a submarine which was monitoring the activity on the Argentine airfields. The messages they sent were called a Shutter report. The signal gave limited information, but it faithfully reported the departure of all Argentine aircraft from their airfields. We discovered that the flying time between the Argentine bases and the Falklands was just over an hour. So when the signal came with the word Shutter you knew that aircraft would be attacking you within the hour. We could see on our radar the Argentine aircraft

Argentinean aircraft in San Carlos.

closing on one side and on the other side the Harriers coming from the Task Force. Because the Argentines were flying high we saw the dogfight as the aircraft met each other, but occasionally one or two enemy aircraft got away and they would head straight for San Carlos Water. Once they'd avoided the Harriers, it was a certainty that we would be attacked. It was my job to keep morale up and inform the ship's company what was happening. I tried to keep my voice calm and report exactly what was happening as and when it occurred.

Although I must admit my heart sank when we had a Shutter report but it galvanized the ship's company into immediate action.

Thirty minutes after we re-anchored in San Carlos the first air attack commenced. A total of 72 Argentine aircraft attacked the ships in the San Carlos anchorage that day; 25 attacked *Intrepid* alone. It was our supreme test, we had trained and trained and always kept the ship's company informed, now we would see if we had done enough.

The first enemy aircraft downed was a dual hit by Seacats from *Intrepid* and the frigate *Plymouth*.

The air attacks came as no surprise but their ferocity did and San Carlos Water soon had the deserved name of Bomb Alley. Bombs were falling all around us, but none hit. We fired at everything with everything we had. We had machine guns and

Near miss on ammunition ship.

Bofors.

rifles manned by Royal Marines down both sides of the ship. We knew of an Argentine attack well before the aircraft reached us as the marines would start firing way before they arrived. The highly skilled pilots flew so low that they were below the Bridge, which was 82 feet above the water.

A pattern of bombs was dropped 100 feet on the Port bow drawing everyone's eyes to that side of the ship, when suddenly a Mirage appeared out of nowhere on the starboard side, swooping over the hill and approaching us fast. My PWO felt we should surely be hit, time literally stood still, but yet again training and delegation saved us. The Sea Cat aimer based on the starboard side had kept his eyes in the right place and fired just at the right time. While he did not down the plane, he caused the pilot to swerve away from us, ditching his bomb load behind the hill.

Another stick of four bombs was dropped on the ship. They missed, just, but three went off and the ship rocked. Those below decks heard something mctallic hit the side of the ship. Was it the fourth bomb which, luckily for us, had not been fused properly and didn't explode?

In spite of *Intrepid*'s personal good fortune the Task Force had suffered losses. *HMS Ardent* was sunk, *Antrim* and *Argonaut* hit, and bombs had hit the *LSL Sir Galahad*.

On that first day of the Argentine bombing raids *HMS Argonaut* had been doing a brilliant job carrying forces to many locations and controlling the air defence. About two hours into the attacks the frigate was hit by one bomb that went through the Bridge and stopped in the ship's magazine where ammunition is stored. Another ended up in the boiler room. Luckily, both these bombs failed to explode. However, several fires started and it is typical of the spirit on board that ship that one of the ratings continued to broadcast on the airways of the local aircraft defence control until he mentioned nonchalantly: 'I'll have to go off for a while. The ship's on fire and smoke is coming under the door.' About 30 minutes later he came back on air saying: 'Fires are out. I'm resuming my defence control commentary now.'

Sea Cat firing.

One of Intrepid's four landing craft taking Scots Guards to Bluff Cove.

Harrier taking off from Atlantic Conveyor.

The bombs, both British-made but sold to the Argentines in more peaceful times, were defused but it took a long time to bring them out. The bomb disposal team was based in *Intrepid*, so we heard about them lowering the bombs over the side and placing them on the sea bed, which is called *the float test,* and is the normal way to dispose of bombs.

As *Argonaut* was too badly damaged to continue the fight she was ordered home. It is customary to put up steam in the engines four or five hours before sailing in order to test the shaft and the turning of the propellers. There seemed to be a massive vibration coming from the shafts so they sent a diver down to check things out. The wire attached to the bomb had wrapped itself around the propellers, and turning them was bringing the bomb right under the ship. Not a position of choice.

Divers had to be sent down to free the bomb from the wire. This was a very dangerous manoeuvre, but their skill ensured a successful outcome.

On 22 May during the raids *Antelope* a type 21 frigate was hit.

There were 20 raids on 23 May. *Fearless* and *Norland* were hit by canon fire. Unexploded bombs were lodged in two LSLs and we gave sanctuary to 160 crew and embarked forces from one of them *Sir Galahad* whilst her bomb was dealt with.

On 25 May, 29 raids came in. As if this constant barrage was not enough, the news got worse. First we heard that *HMS Coventry*, sister ship to *Sheffield*, had been sunk whilst in company with *HMS Broadsword* acting as decoys to draw Argentine aircraft away from Bomb Alley. This was a very low moment for us all. Then a

Atlantic Conveyor *with another Harrier being launched.*

further signal arrived saying *Atlantic Conveyor* had been hit by two Exocet missiles and sunk. Her loss was not just a tragedy and a huge blow to confidence, it also meant we lost her cargo of, three Chinook helicopters, eight Wessex helicopters, other transport vehicles, runway building equipment to enable the Harriers to operate from ashore, tents and essential logistics for the land force, which forced the commanders to switch to more amphibious operations than had been anticipated. Fortunately, all the Harriers and one Chinook were flying, so escaped to provide air cover and limited but crucial heavy lift at key stages of the land battle.

I truly believed that the ship's company could not take another loss at that moment. I instructed my Commander that this information should be withheld for about an hour to allow them all to digest and come to terms with the bad news they already had. I allowed the knowledge to circulate in a general manner an hour or so later, and it was accepted without comment.

On 25 May there were five raids. We looked after 223 crew from *Antelope* as, whilst her unexploded bomb was being defused, the bomb had exploded killing the bomb disposal expert and another crew member and causing fires to rage through the ship. These eventually reached the missiles and munitions store and the ship blew up and sank.

Throughout the raids I had the ship's main broadcast in my hand and as events occurred I relayed them to the ship's company. This I was to do while under attack until the end of hostilities some 24 days later. I know we formed an unbreakable bond. They knew my voice, knew they were going to be told the truth of the attack and also, importantly, the gossip. I would indicate the threatened side of the ship when possible so they were prepared in every way. In my last broadcast of that first day I reminded the ship's company of the words spoken by Admiral Cunningham*, after heavy losses in the Mediterranean: *'It takes three hundred years to build a tradition but only three years to build a ship.'* I told the ship's company that I felt they were now part of that tradition.

I was fortunate enough to have two Chaplains on board. One was normally ashore with the landing forces. The other I asked to wander around the ship the whole time, requiring acts of bravery from him in the more confined areas. On one occasion I broadcast an Air Raid Warning Red with an added note of advice 'to hit the deck'. The Padre and the group with him were praying several decks down, and as they dropped he said in a clear voice: 'Good Lord, protect us!' then fell silent. A sailor lying close by gave him a smart jab in the ribs and said: 'For God's sake don't stop praying now!' He hastily resumed his prayers, aloud. This incident went round the ship in seconds and provided some well needed humour…

The threat of underwater swimmers placing grenades or mines on the sides or bottom of the ships was another concern. When at anchor we dropped a charges of approx 1lb of explosive over the side on a regular basis, they would fall a little way then explode, putting off we hoped, any saboteurs. The frequency of these drops depended on how high we felt the risk. Whether they existed or were ghostly imaginings, I have no idea, but we did shoot a lot of black plastic bags, which bear an uncanny resemblance to the head of an underwater swimmer.

There were various intercepts of Argentine communications – the most notable was someone hidden in the hills opposite San Carlos, who could see every ship arriving and leaving and could therefore monitor all movements. We could hear his broadcasts and knew they should be stopped. We sent a landing craft to the area and about 20 marines swept through searching for him. They scoured the likeliest zones but couldn't find him. We listened to him relaying the search to his masters, telling them that the soldiers had missed his hideout. In fact we never found him. He was a very brave man. I hope he was rewarded for his courage.

27 May – 4 June: Break out from the beachhead

The plan was to establish a secure beachhead around San Carlos Water from which to mount offensive operations, and then re-capture Darwin and Goose Green before advancing and re-taking Port Stanley. 3 Commando Brigade would advance on Stanley through the northern half of East Falkland whilst 5 Infantry Brigade, who were to land later, would advance through the southern half.

As a Task Force we had achieved our first objective; we were ashore and, although we were now taking the brunt of enemy attack, we were shooting down their aircraft.

What followed was the break out from the San Carlos beachhead by 3 Commando Brigade, the landing of 5 Infantry Brigade and the subsequent land operations to re-take Port Stanley and thus the Islands.

In amphibious operations the doctrine is that the approach to the amphibious operating area (AOA) and landing is a naval operation. The commander of the amphibious task force, in this case Commodore Clapp, embarked with his headquarters in *HMS Fearless*. At an appropriate moment when both the naval and land commanders agree that sufficient force has been built up ashore, the amphibious operation is formerly terminated and command is passed to the land force commander, in this case Brigadier Thompson, the Commander of 3 Commando Brigade, Royal Marines. That moment occurred at 6pm local time on 27 May.

In this case the Commodore handed over control to the land force sooner than planned or actually correct by the drill book, in order to collect Major General Moore Royal Marines, who was to assume overall command of all forces, and 5 Brigade from the *QE2* in South Georgia. This transfer was to be completed as soon as possible in order to brief the Major General. Commodore Clapp was extremely concerned at the lack of information Moore was receiving, not due to any personnel failings but to the failure of *QE2*'s satellite communication system.

After an absence of four days the Commodore and *HMS Fearless* returned to San Carlos Water, where Moore and 5 Brigade disembarked. Commodore Clapp had left me in charge of naval activities in San Carlos Water in his absence.

From this point on in the operation, *Intrepid* really came into her own, as we exploited our knowledge and experience and demonstrated such flexibility in support of operations ashore that even its designers might have been stretched to imagine. We stayed in San Carlos during the day, for the next 25 days, and sailed at night to carry out insertions of SAS/SBS and later with troops and logistics towards the South and Fitzroy as well as a couple of other excursions. The ideal was to get back into the moderately protective cover of San Carlos before daylight. If we did not make it back by then the fate of *HMS Ardent* awaited us. Caution was the watchword.

Overnight on 26/27 May *Intrepid* sailed round to Salvador Waters in the north east to insert SBS patrols by rigid raiding craft to recce the settlement at Teal Inlet. The plan was that this area would be established as a forward maintenance area for 3 Commando Brigade later on and for 5 Army Brigade to follow through using the same store dumps and ammo.

On another night incursion, we were ordered to drop a small party of SAS on a beach near an island suspected of being an airfield. The Argentines had taken the top of a field, cut some grass and just moved some versatile planes there, which could have done untold damage as they were small and nippy. It was decided they should be removed, so out from the flooded dock came a group of flat boats containing the SAS to carry out the action. They touched the beach and slithered on to shore. As they looked up from their prone positions they saw the silhouettes of five people on the horizon. Their first thought was "God, we've been rumbled!" and they remained in position for a further 20 minutes. The enemy still hadn't moved an inch, so the SAS decided to rush them. Five very startled penguins moved off at speed! The SAS got on with their delayed action. These incidents were not without their humour, on one occasion, we docked the ship down, lowered the stern gate and out came two canoes, paddling away. We must have looked a very frightening invasion force.

27/28/29 May: 2 Para with artillery support approached and attacked Goose Green. During the attack, Lt Col H Jones, the CO of 2 Para was killed whilst assaulting an Argentine position. His action broke a deadlock and led to the surrender of the Argentine garrison that outnumbered the Paras by nearly 2:1. He was awarded a posthumous VC. On board *Intrepid* we monitored the whole battle, powerless to help but willing them to succeed.

On 27 May 45 Commando and 3 Para started their march across the moorland terrain towards the coastal settlements of Douglas and Teal Inlet respectively. After slow progress, due to the terrain and heavy loads, both settlements were secured late on 28 May.

42 Commando prepared to be ferried to Mount Kent by helicopter. Thankfully, this operation was preceded by several days of intense patrolling activity by the SAS and 3 Commando Brigade's Mountain and Arctic Warfare Cadre (M&AWC), who engaged Argentine special forces who, unbeknownst to planners in UK who wanted 42 Commando to be flown forward without detailed reconnaissance, had been

Hermes off the Falklands.

positioned in order to tie down our advance. After weather delays and in spite of the paucity of helicopters, the move started on 31 May.

On 30 May I was ordered to join the main fleet – *HMS Hermes, Invincible*, a great many Royal Fleet Auxiliary (RFAs) and a variety of frigates – which was cleverly stationed about 100 miles east of the Falklands. This well chosen location ensured that the fleet had plenty of time to position itself if it came under attack, and was also the minimum distance for the Harriers, if they were to intercept enemy aircraft before they hit San Carlos.

We were taking a Lynx helicopter to *HMS Brilliant* for repair by the fleet engineers. We set sail from San Carlos and, on the way to join the Fleet, we enjoyed a superb day, discussing how nice it was to have some open sea time rather than being surrounded by the claustrophobic hills of San Carlos.

On joining the fleet, we were given a station and moved across into position. Suddenly the dread word "Handbrake!" came across the airwaves. This heralded enemy action which had been picked up following the detection of a Mirage radar. Sure enough two Mirage jets came roaring in and fired two Exocet missiles at us. The first failed to acquire a target, the second was shot down by either a Type 42 frigate firing a Sea Dart or a Type 21 frigate firing a gun. We will never know who had the battle honours, as they both claimed victory. We were just grateful that one of them managed a bull's eye.

*   *   *   *   *

Admiral Sandy Woodward (Commander Carrier Battle Group) created a communication channel which enabled him to speak directly to all the Commanders of his Task Group. After this onslaught, a familiar voice came over the airwaves. 'How did you like that lot Hugh?' Another familiar voice replied: 'I could do without a repetition of that, thanks!' with a chuckle. Hearing those familiar voices on line, gave us great comfort, as we had gone through our careers in the navy together and been friends for a very long time. This technology allowed Admiral Woodward's Band of Brothers immediate access to their Admiral, whereas Nelson's Band of Brothers had had to travel a good distance by small boat to *HMS Victory*, in order to be briefed by their Admiral.

On the way back to San Carlos the next day I was very low on fuel. You had to take your chance to refuel when you could, as weather conditions could be horrific, and running out of fuel was not an option. It took four hours at the side of the tanker to refuel. You are only 120 feet apart and in rough seas that is about as close as you want to get.

After being alongside for two hours, we suddenly got word that Mirage radar had been detected. The voice of approaching doom came over the airwaves and we had no idea where the attack was coming from, so we got rid of the fuel lines and

Intrepid *refuelling in bad weather.*

hoses attaching us, pronto. As we spiraled round, one turned to starboard and one to port, we fired off our rocket launchers, covering a huge area in chaff which would hopefully protect us from any incoming Exocets. It was pretty tense on the Bridge, when a loud and angry voice came over the airwaves: 'Will someone please tell me what the bloody hell is going on?' It was a frigate about 5 miles behind us. Neither of us knew the other was there. He'd just seen all the rockets going off, so we stopped shooting. The Bridge creased up with nervous laughter and the tension was over. We never did find out where the Mirages got to but we arrived safely in San Carlos before daylight. After this little trip it was a moot point with the ship's company as to which was worse, Bomb Alley or Exocet country.

Overnight on 31 May/1 June our Heath Robinson-look minesweeper came into its own when we were ordered to ensure that the possible route into Teal Inlet for stores and ammunition was clear of mines. We headed north east again to Teal Inlet, this time a lot closer in than before. We docked down (filled the dock with water), which was quite a dangerous process a scant half a mile from potential enemy forces, and the two landing craft launched off into their mine seeking mission.

The two corporals driving the Mine Counter Measures (MCM) landing craft were extremely brave men. They knew that if they set off a mine they would have been blown to pieces. But these two dragged this makeshift minesweeping gear up and down Teal Inlet twice.

The following night 1/2 June we returned to Salvador Waters to recover the MCM team. The landing craft corporal signalled me, asking what to do with the magnets. I said 'Ditch them,' which they did. So somewhere buried in the bottom of an inlet in the north of the Falklands are two large magnets producing a strong magnetic anomaly.

On their return I asked one of the corporals, 'Did you see us disappearing into the mist?' His reply made me shudder. 'No disappearance, Sir. You stood out like a dog's bollocks, Sir! The moon lit you up beautifully; you were very clear from everywhere, Sir!'

This episode with its black humour brought to mind an incident from my family archives during the Second World War, when my mother was guarding our village streets as an Air Raid Warden, my father was away at sea in the Royal Navy, and my grandfather doing his bit by joining the Home Guard. My grandfather was a very tall man, over 6ft 5in, so whoever decided that he would make a good watcher for enemy landings, in a small dug out in one of the hawthorn hedges which lined the route from the south downs to Sea, must have been thinking of a future episode of *Dad's Army*.

Even bent double he was very conspicuous, but as he had been ordered to stay in this place should the invasion occur and, then report on any enemy positions and activities, he obediently took on this role, even though any self respecting German invader would have spotted him a mile away!

After our MCM excursion we were ordered to what was known as the deep field, or the whimsically named TRALA (Tug Repair and Logistic Area) to replenish stores, collect mail and rest. Some hope of the latter with two more Exocet alerts! Later we found out that the attack on the Carrier Battle Group that we'd been caught up in on 30 May used the last of the air-dropped Exocets.

One of the most popular helicopter pilots was the one who dropped our mail. Mail meant an enormous amount to all serving in the fleet. One of my best deliveries was a badly wrapped parcel from my mother, as it reminded me of the equally badly wrapped parcels I used to watch her complete for my father when he was serving in the Indian Ocean in the Second World War. Inside mine was the local village paper, a jar of marmite and other goodies. The sheer ordinariness of the contents was an enormous comfort.

4–12 June: The advance on Port Stanley

Intrepid returned unmolested to San Carlos Water on 4 June. Soon the land forces commenced their rapid progress towards Port Stanley. Major General Moore had arrived to take overall command of the land battle and 5 Infantry Brigade* made up from – 2 Scots Guards, 1 Welsh Guards, 1/7 Ghurka Rifles and Artillery, engineer and light helicopter support had begun landing in San Carlos. 5 Brigade had no integral logistic support so the Commando Logistic Regiment had to support both Brigades. 2 Para transferred from 3 Commando Brigade to 5 Infantry Brigade.

In the north, 3 Commando Brigade made up from 42 and 45 Commandos and 2 Para consolidated positions around Mounts Estancia, Kent and Challenger, within artillery range of Argentine guns, and began patrolling towards Mount Longdon, Two Sisters and Mount Harriet in preparation for the final attack on Stanley. 40 Commando remained at San Carlos as Force Reserve. The Brigade headquarters moved to their forward base at Teal Inlet that *Intrepid* had opened up earlier.

In the south the plan was to move as quickly as possible to the southern approaches to Stanley through Fitzroy, which had been designated as the site of the forward maintenance area for 5 Brigade. 1/7 Ghurka Rifles were helicoptered to Goose Green and an advance party of 2 Para flew forward to Swan Inlet House where, by the simple expedient of phoning ahead, they established that Fitzroy and Bluff Cove were clear of enemy. 2 Para then flew forward and occupied those settlements.

This unexpected move by 2 Para left the southern flank quite exposed. The replacement helicopters for those lost in the *Atlantic Conveyor* had not arrived so, in the absence of sufficient helicopter lift, Major General Moore decided to move the two Guards battalions forward by sea. The initial plan was for half the Welsh Guards to start marching light whilst the other half and the Scots Guards, together with all their equipment, would be ferried in *Intrepid* and *Sir Tristram* one of the Landing Ship's Logistics (LSLs) overnight on 5/6 June. They would unload next day. Neither battalion had any experience or training in amphibious operations.

Political pressure from the UK forced the Commodore to alter the plan. It was considered too risky to commit the LPDs to daylight offloads so close to Argentine forces, so a more complicated operation was planned. The LPDs would each sail on consecutive nights to the vicinity of Lively Island from where their embarked troops would be ferried forward to Fitzroy in their LCUs. An LSL would follow each and the LCUs would be used to offload them before being picked up again a night later by their parent LPD. Each excursion would be escorted appropriately.

Meanwhile half the Welsh Guards had set out on their unexpected 20-mile tab, to Fitzroy. Army units tab, Royal Marines units yomp, both meaning to walk with a heavy load over difficult terrain. The Welsh Guards attempted to do so fully laden, perhaps being unwilling to travel light and separated from their equipment. Unlike the Commandos and Paras they had been unable to achieve the high levels of fitness on their journey from the UK that were necessary to complete this arduous journey

143

successfully. They had expected to be assigned to garrison duties and had not been prepared sufficiently for action. After six miles, they turned back exhausted to San Carlos and were landed at Bluff Cove a few days later.

On 5 June *Intrepid* was duly deployed to take the Scots Guards to Fitzroy. This had not been the original plan, but the loss of *Atlantic Conveyor**, which carried Harriers and both Wessex and Chinook helicopters, caused major problems to the planned transport of both men and logistics.

My instructions were quite clear: conduct fast passage to Lively Sound, extract landing craft and return San Carlos Water by first light.

These are the actual orders for this incursion.
OPERATION CORPORATE-NIGHT INTENTIONS 5th/6th June
1. No convoy in either direction (from San Carlos to the Carriers).
2. **Intrepid** and **Penelope** sail at last light as ordered **Intrepid** conduct fast passage to Lively Sound, extract landing craft and return San Carlos Water by first light.
3. **Avenger** sail at last light, conduct fast passage to Sea Lion Island for Naval Gunfire Support Naval Gunfire Support on airstrip. When **Intrepid** past retire to west for 1 hour before **Intrepid** passes on return leg until 30 minutes after. Join **Penelope** and **Intrepid** for return passage San Carlos Water.
4. **Arrow** sail San Carlos Water as required R/V **Sir Galahad** vicinity Big Shag at 060400z. Escort **Sir Galahad** to San Carlos by first light.
5. **Plymouth** and **Exeter** patrol North end of Falkland Sound as ordered. **Exeter**, **Plymouth** remain between tide rock and line joining North West Island and Many Branch Point. Exeter adjust station to maintain communications with rapier batteries.
6. **Fearless, Sir Lancelet, Sir Geraint, Sir Tristram, Blue Rover, Nordic ferry Elk** remain San Carlos Water.

The route we took had never been used by a big ship. It was a very difficult trip but I had enormous confidence in my brilliant navigator. On board we had 500 ship's company and 800 Scots Guards, as well as numerous hangers on. We also had a Marine Major, who was in charge of disembarking the Scots Guards at their destination. He knew both the coastline and waters very well as he had previously sailed his yacht in the area, as part of the Royal Marine Attachment based on the Falkland Islands. With his great knowledge of the local area and his expertise in handling landing craft, he was the perfect man to get his charges, the Scots Guards, ashore as quickly, efficiently and safely as possible.

Before we had even left San Carlos, it had been mooted that we take the Scots Guards up to Elephant Island, a further 18 miles up the coast towards Stanley. As this would have involved me taking *Intrepid* across the land-based Exocet zone, I was unhappy with these proposals.

The land-based Exocet zone was a serious danger to ships. The first firing occurred on 5 June and narrowly missed a frigate at the edge of the Exocet zone. If I had dropped the Scots Guards further up the coast, *Intrepid* would have been an attractive and large target for those operating this missile. Luckily for us it took the operators some time to work out how to use it effectively, but when they did they later hit and seriously damaged *HMS Glamorgan*. Also a longer journey that night to get to Elephant Island would have involved *Intrepid* returning to San Carlos in daylight. The loss of both men and *LSL Sir Galahad* and damage done to *LSL Sir Tristram* tragically showed what happened to amphibious ships outside the shelter of San Carlos Water in daylight.

The second option was to disembark off Lively Island, just short of the land-based Exocet zone. There were two reasons I felt it was impossible on the day.

Firstly there was a large swell running, which would prevent the landing craft extracting safely from *Intrepid*, but large swells occur in a calm sea and cause the landing craft to knock together in the dock. This is both dangerous and uncomfortable for the men inside them.

Most importantly, when the stern gate was lowered and the dock flooded to float the landing craft, the ship had to remain on that course for a minimum of 40 minutes, at a maximum speed of 4 knots going forwards, while she was de-ballasted. With a huge swell to deal with as well, this could take even longer and would leave the ship very vulnerable to attack. *Intrepid* was not the most agile of creatures and could not be manoeuvred speedily. If I was going to be able to disembark the landing craft safely I had to find shelter away from the swell. I had no intention of making my ship, my ship's company or the Scots Guards on board, sitting ducks.

My navigator and I discussed the possibilities and we decided on Lively Sound situated on the eastern side of Lively Island. This position offered us calm water for disembarkation.

It meant that the Scots Guards would have a much longer journey in small open craft on a rough sea and they would also have to cross the land-based Exocet zone. My reasoning was that, due to their size, an Exocet would cause no threat to their safety, as it was highly unlikely they would be picked up by the enemy radar, which was a large land-based radar in Stanley.

The Marine Major in charge of the disembarkation had very strong feelings about the distance he and his men would have to travel; however, I knew that it

Uganda, *the Hospital Ship.*

would be politically unacceptable to lose an LPD such as *Intrepid*, particularly with a battalion of infantry embarked. Although I was willing to do anything and take many risks, and did, driving my ship knowingly into an Exocet zone was not one of them. With the amount of mixed forces on board it would have been carnage if we had been hit.

Suffice to say that it boiled down to the classic amphibious dichotomy between naval and land imperatives. On the one hand, the safety of the ship and embarked force is paramount and, on the other, the need to land as close to the objective as possible takes precedence. That always requires compromise, but ultimately it is a naval responsibility to land the landing force.

The troops had a very uncomfortable and wet eight-hour voyage to Fitzroy and, despite their safe arrival, their trip was not without further incident, as a British frigate coming off the gun line detected four echoes closing the coast, which they thought might be Argentine reinforcements. Fortunately, the senior officer, who was about to give the order to open fire, decided something did not look right, so ordered the firing of star shells to check the targets. These illuminated the four landing craft and they were recognized as British. In his report of the incident later, the senior officer said, 'I felt the hairs on the back of my neck stand on end!' So thank goodness they did.

Our LCUs stayed behind and ferried 2 Para to Fitzroy. We, on the other hand, steamed back at 18 knots and under cover of darkness to San Carlos Water. On our return journey, just as we entered the Falkland Sound, the engine room reported a major defect in one of our engines. I was offered two options, proceed at 18 knots and possibly cause irreparable damage, or come down to 10 knots, nursing the engines until we arrived in San Carlos. At 10 knots we were a sitting duck for enemy action, so there really was no option, we steamed on at 18 knots and slipped into San Carlos Water just before sunrise. Repairs were completed in 24 hours. I have set out below a passage from my passage report.

Passage Report
On June 5 we weighed anchor at 20.30 and sailed from San Carlos at 18 knots. Our route took us through the Falkland Sound, Eagle Passage then headed towards Lively Island which fell just outside the land-based Exocet danger zone positioned by Stanley.

Avenger was ordered to make fast passage ahead to conduct naval gunfire support, as one of the islands we were passing had an airstrip and we wanted the Argentines to be more interested in *Avenger* damaging their airstrip than *Intrepid*'s passage.

Argentinian aircraft refuelling.

Penelope was given loose station two or three miles ahead of *Intrepid* and was in charge of all coordination duties. *Exeter* sailed to station at Seal Island. Only navigational radar was used, otherwise all was silence.

At 20.40: air raid warnings given on three contacts 30 miles to the west. These are classified as spurious at 20.47 and the ship reverts to warning Yellow, a lower state of readiness.

21.10: *Intrepid* reverts from 'action stations' to 'defence stations'. One Bofors is manned. We proceed south down the Sound. The land to starboard is enemy held.

21.20: lights from a vehicle seen at Green 30.

21.22: *Avenger* reports lights on an unidentified road to starboard.

This is evaluated as the Argentine Hospital ship *Valparaiso* based in Port Howard. She should have sailed earlier; is she monitoring and reporting our movements?

As we approach the Straits, *Avenger* moves further west to give more gunfire support.

23.15: *Penelope* reports we are being illuminated by fire control radar, from the shore in the vicinity of Tatis Bay.

23.45: first gunfire report from *Avenger* just 20 miles astern from us.

00.00: Sea Lion Island is 20 miles on the port bow. Intelligence has suggested that aircraft are possibly based there.

00.29: Argentine C130 is reported in the vicinity of the Falklands. We have been ordered not to engage with the enemy so as not to draw attention to ourselves.

01.30: the enemy aircraft returns to her base.

04.50: we report to *Avenger* that we would soon be passing Sea Lion Island.

06.00: we return to San Carlos Water as daylight breaks.

Overnight on 6/7 June *Fearless* made the same trip with the Welsh Guards but with only two landing crafts on board could land only part of the battalion and brought the rest back to San Carlos to be cross-decked and to be landed from *Sir Galahad* on 8 June.

On the evening of June 7/8 *Intrepid* repeated the journey to pick up our LCUs. Unloading and reloading was completed at 04.16 and we commenced our return at 12 knots, then speeded up to 18 knots, with no other incidents, heading back to San Carlos Water. I have set out another extract from a passage report.

Passage Report

On the evening of June7/8 *Intrepid* repeats the journey in the company of *Plymouth* and *Cardiff*, on duty in the Sound. We pass her just south of the Sound.

At **23.59** *Minerva* reports a radar transmission on the starboard side. This is again reported at 00.05. A cross cut puts the radar on speed with Speedwell Island. Confidence in these rackets is low, but as a precaution hands are called to action stations at **00.27**. At **00.46** *Minerva* is ordered to launch a Lynx helicopter to carry out a search east of Speedwell Island and then ahead of the ships. The Lynx is launched at **01.23**. At the same time a shuttle report is received of impending enemy aircraft approaching.

Minerva does not try to jam the enemy radar, so as not to give a beacon, but she reports an Argentine system has acquired *Minerva*'s Lynx helicopter which remains low as the hostiles pass overhead. Hostiles are assumed to be high because of the high detecting ranges.

Intrepid uses snow showers to reduce chances of visual radar detection when the aircraft flies very close. The aircraft are now identified as three pairs, two within ten miles of each other coming towards us and the third pair passing 20 miles north and eventually closing Stanley from the south.

At **01.34** the leading pair of aircraft turn to the north east and make a landfall in the vicinity of Speedwell heading towards troop positions. The raid to the south passes off at **01.39** showing IF at 44 and 16 miles.

At **01.49** a large glow is observed in the sky. Possibly an aircraft hit.

An aircraft is reported inbound from the east at **01.42**.

Aircraft begin clearing the area at **01.52** passing eight miles astern of *Intrepid* and coming and opening.

The **British LCMs** are identified on radar at **03.03** and *Minerva* closes to identify positively. At **03.39** during the approach of the **LCMs** a thermal glare is seen in the direction of the land. Three-inch rockets are fired in case of an Exocet firing. We begin unloading the LCM's at **03.42**. Unloading and reloading is completed at **04.16** and we commence our return at 12 knots, speeding up to 18 knots, with no other incidents, heading back to San Carlos Water.

These night runs demonstrated again the burden of command in terms of fatigue. In one period I was not to go to bed for 72 hours. For as soon as we had completed our nightly insertions we had to be ready to face air attack in San Carlos. My navigator also had to face the problem of fatigue. My Commander, who was so essential in maintaining the overall morale of the ship and ensuring the ship was able to cope with many conflicting requirements while in San Carlos, ranging from casualties to bomb disposal and who, therefore, could not provide relief if he was to carry out his own duties properly, stated that his most fervent wish was: '... that the Captain and the navigator don't fall asleep at the same time!' A constant supply of bacon sandwiches proved to be a most helpful remedy to exhaustion.

INTREPID's FALKLAND PRAYER
This irreverent parody featured in the Newssheet produced by *Intrepid* which appeared every couple of days.

"Our Captain who art in the Ops Room,
Dingemans be his Name,
The Mirages come, they will be splashed,
Overland and over sea,
Give us this day our Daily Sitrep,
And forgive those who fire Sea Cat against us,
Lead us not into Super Entendard country,
And protect us from Exocet,
For thine is the CAP, the Sea Dart and the Rapier,
Onward to Deep Clean."

* * * * *

On 8 June both *Sirs Tristram* and *Galahad* were off Fitzroy unloading in daylight. By early afternoon all but the Welsh Guards had been put ashore. The guards wanted to be taken to Bluff Cove as a short cut to a seven-mile tab around the head of the bay over a bridge that was possibly impassable. They were told that this could not be achieved and in one of those awful, unintended consequences – this time their lack of experience and training in amphibious operations they refused to disembark. Tragically the ships had been spotted and were bombed, leading to 48 dead and 115 wounded.

Casualties and crew from both ships were flown to *Intrepid* and from 9 to 12 June we hosted 200 Welsh Guards survivors for re-equipping.

Whilst the Guards were recovering from the attack on *Sir Galahad*, my electronic warfare experts rushed in and said: 'You'd better look at this, Sir.' All we could decipher from the intercepted Argentine signal was the phrase *gas gas gas*. It could have been some harmless reference but we weren't sure. I sent a Flash Signal to the Commander in Chief and the MoD. We closed the ship down and put on our gas masks. Within seconds the Commander of the Welsh Guards came rushing up and put a reasonable question to me. 'Why haven't my team been given gas masks?' I replied that we only carried a few surplus and they had been distributed. 'Right Sir' came his reply, 'we're getting off.' The Welsh Guards disembarked as swiftly as possible to dry land. I didn't really blame them.

Our last test was to be on 12 June the day before the Argentine surrender. During one of the nightly insertions, I had just reached the open sea south of East Falkland when an incoming raid was detected at 134 miles, closing at 500 knots. I immediately took to the airwaves, informing anyone and everyone in the task force listening, that we were about to come under attack. The raid was on a steady bearing, which meant that the aircraft would pass right above us. We had no blind fire capability, so I told the ship's company that we would turn *Intrepid* to face the aircraft and would fire everything we had into the sky and trust to luck. At the last minute, the aircraft changed course and passed three miles astern, luckily for us. This was followed by another group of hostiles approaching and we quickly closed the coast. There, we were fortunate enough to stumble across a convenient snow storm, where we hoped we could not be seen and in which we circled the ship until the aircraft were well clear. Our supposed safety was short lived and ineffective, as my Spanish interpreters who were listening to the traffic between aircraft heard one say to the other, 'We've just flown over two warships, let's go back and get them' and they started to bank toward us. Just when we thought our luck had run out the lead aircraft was hit by a Sea Dart fired from *Cardiff* at 28 miles. The other disappeared home. About ten miles away, *Glamorgan* was hit and badly damaged by the land-based Exocet that had given me nightmares.

In our Operations Room we had a large board on which we place every known enemy Exocet where they were and how they had been used. At the end of the war we reckoned there were two left.

By close of play on 12 June, 3 Commando Brigade was in possession of Mount Longdon, Two Sisters and Mount Harriet, overlooking Port Stanley.

13–25 June: Surrender and aftermath

By dawn on 14 June, 5 Infantry Brigade was in possession of Wireless Ridge and Tumbledown. During the course of the day Argentine forces began falling back on Port Stanley from the other positions on Mount William and Sapper Hill that were about to be attacked. There was then a race to the outskirts of Stanley where British forces halted whilst surrender was negotiated. Major General Moore flew into Stanley and accepted the surrender of all Argentine forces from General Menendez at 9.30pm local time on 14 June.

*   *   *   *   *

At the end of a war, you cannot just pack up and go home. There is a tremendous amount of clearing up to do of both men and logistics. As victors we were also responsible for the prisoners of war.

One of the first jobs we were given was to go to Port Howard to collect one thousand Argentine prisoners.

The second group of prisoners was at Fox Bay. We hoped to transfer them in landing craft, but there was a huge swell running and, as I have already said, using landing craft in a swell makes it dangerous and very uncomfortable for those travelling in them. We decided to wait overnight and hope the swell was less substantial in the morning. We anchored and I went to bed, only to be woken in the night by the Officer of the Watch with a grim message: 'Sir, we are losing all power.' During the night we had swung over huge swathes of kelp (seaweed), and they were gradually blocking our seawater inlets. As a consequence there was no cooling water going to our generators.

We had two generators and as the seaweed enveloped our inlets the lights were going out all over the ship. One generator was still working but if that packed up we were in serious trouble; with no power on board we would be unable to move. I decided we had better get out of the seaweed as quickly as possible. The anchor had four cables out and I knew that our one chance was to haul the ship away from the seaweed by slowly hauling in cable. We did not dare use the engines to break out before we got the inlets unblocked and working again.

We started to haul in the anchor, and although we had to take it very slowly, the temptation to rush it was appealing, as the ship was very nearly in complete darkness and everyone on board was beginning to wonder what was going on. Just as dawn was breaking, we were greeted by a shaft of light, electric light, right the way through the ship. The inlets were free and lights were back on. We had made it.

Over 1000 Argentine soldiers, a whole regiment, were embarked by helicopter as the swell had not died down enough for it to be safe to transport them in LCUs from the shore in West Falklands to the ship. *Avenger* had been allocated to help get the prisoners aboard and her Captain called me up to say that all the prisoners had been transferred to *Intrepid* except for the regimental dog. He asked whether it should be shot. My reply was quick: 'We've just won the war, if we shoot it we'll probably start another.' So the next helicopter drop was one large regimental mascot, a Husky.

The ordinary soldiers who arrived on board were terrified, they imagined we were going to shoot them. Whilst their officers and senior NCOs had lived a life of luxury ashore with as much food and drink as they wanted, they were cold and hungry and had not had a decent hot meal for weeks. We ensured they were given hot food and hot drinks, although this gave many of them stomach problems, which left us with an unpleasant cleaning up problem once they had been transferred.

Their Colonel had no interest in their well being – only his own. The moment he arrived on board, he demanded to see his own accommodation. He never asked to see his men, nor did he enquire about their well being. His only worry was for the safety of two small pearl handle revolvers, which we had confiscated from him. We were all so disgusted by his lack of compassion for his men that we were not saddened by the news that these precious revolvers had somehow become 'lost' at sea.

The prisoners were transferred the next day to *Canberra* and other non military ships and taken home and disembarked in Puerto Madryn. I understand that they were not treated well on their return to Argentina and little or no care was given to these traumatised young men.

*　*　*　*　*

Intrepid acted as a hotel for those ordered to help with the clean up. At one point in San Carlos Water we were anchored near the shore with a submarine, a tanker and a frigate tied up to us. We were being used as laundry, shower room and feeding station. Everyone longed for hot showers and clean clothes.

Throughout the conflict *Intrepid* had been running a laundry as all the kit had to be washed. Most people find the occasional sock in their tumble dryers. But on *Intrepid* with several thousand combat troops and Special Forces coming and going, let alone the ship's company, lost socks were a minor problem. Shrinkage was a real risk as the normal Chinese laundry crew had declined to come to the Falklands, so ordinary seamen were running the show. They soon found that running a laundry during a conflict was not quite the same as in peacetime. Along with small arms and ammunition our best retrieval was a couple of hand grenades that had survived a hot wash and were only discovered after someone heard the deafening noise they made while hurtling around the tumble dryer! It was a small miracle they did not explode.

It was bliss for the ship's company to be out of their Action dress which most had worn continuosly while we were under attack. It started with uniform shirt and trousers, and then came the heavy stiff white gloves and head mask, these were to ensure your hands and head were protected from fire or flash. The gas mask was ever present and speaks for itself. Hanging from your waist was the *once only* suit that you put over everything. It was bright red and would keep you warm should you end up in the water for a couple of hours. I think some of the crew slept in theirs.

*   *   *   *   *

One day I toddled off to my cabin for a nap, to try and catch up on some unbroken sleep, something that I had not enjoyed for a considerable time. I should have known better because I soon received a call from the Officer of the Watch: 'Sir, we're drifting to the shore!' We had just won a war, we had managed to complete our duties with no injuries and very few mishaps. Was this to be the moment that it all went pear shaped? The submarine, the tanker and the frigate were not taking any chances. They dropped their lines and scarpered.

I sent orders to start engines and move out of the danger zone. Although the engines were at immediate notice and I sent the order 'Obey Telegraphs', there was some delay before we could use the engines. The immediate action I had been accustomed to over the last few wartime weeks did not happen. Running aground is not good news for the ship or a good career move for the Captain in charge. She might end up in the scrap yard and he definitely ends up in a Court Martial.

My future life behind bars was flashing through my mind, when they finally acknowledged my order, and with great relief my next order was 'Slow Ahead' and we started to pull away from the shore.

Elderly *Intrepid's* propulsion machinery may have been, but its rugged simplicity proved its worth a thousand fold in the Falklands conflict. Activated after months from a deeply dormant state of minimal maintenance it was sterling work from Portsmouth dockyard and the few *Intrepid* engineers remaining on board, to get her running in ten days and fully functional within a fortnight. Two boilers feeding steam to their respective turbine engine then drove *Intrepid* to the other side of the globe and to war.

Once in action zone, the engines rotated slowly at immediate notice day after day and night after night without faltering. Called to full readiness in minutes, they propelled *Intrepid* at her maximum speed during her forays into the intensely dangerous combat areas to drop off and pick up troops and, as often as not, carry out the duties of a nimbler frigate. There were only two occasions they faltered, and then only briefly: once when an overheating bearing jammed in place whilst being removed and, on another occasion, as the ship dragged her anchor as related above, when her engineers reported a small delay in getting her underway. That with so little maintenance and repair these engines carried us to war and back safely is a tribute to the build and quality of those engines and to those who maintained and operated them.

During the clearing up operations *Intrepid* was used as a floating supply base and hotel for all services to go ashore and help put things back together for the civilian population. This ranged from replacing fencing for livestock to fixing leaky roofs or repainting defaced property. We even had doctors and dentists on board. Our helicopters and boats would zoom off, on a daily basis, taking a variety of technicians and professionals to some near and some very remote locations.

Hearing some of the varied stories from crew and officers, I decided to go on one of these trips to meet the people we had fought for. Not all of them were grateful, some in fact were quite cross at the lack of care their homes and properties had received from the invading army, and even crosser if their property lay in the path of the battles. This attitude, while understandable, was not popular among servicemen who had lost friends in the conflict.

So I joined the next helicopter going on shore. The first house we landed by looked like an old tin hut. As we went inside, I was stunned by the interior, it reminded me of an English cottage in *Homes and Gardens* magazine. It could not have been more English. It made our little visiting group realise what we were doing down there, restoring people's property and sovereignty. I celebrated with our hosts by having the first whisky I had tasted for three months.

Our next stop was at a very isolated farm in the West Falklands. This particular farmer welcomed us to his home and was extremely grateful for the assistance. He had originally come from New Zealand and had moved to this very isolated spot to farm beef and sheep. There was no whisky on the menu this time, but coffee and a chat round the kitchen table. We conversed, while the technicians completed the works, and he was very keen for us to stay on for a meal, as I believe he was very lonely, but we had to move on to other jobs.

Our leave-taking was delayed when the farmer rushed out and said: 'Hang on a minute, would you please take something back to the ship for me?' and proceeded to rush round the corner, before I had time to speak.

As space was at a premium on board *Intrepid*, I was dreading being asked to take some huge family heirloom back to the UK. Two minutes later, a tractor towing a trailer whizzed up to the helicopter and, there in the trailer, was the most enormous side of beef. 'I thought you boys might fancy some fresh meat,' grinned the farmer.

We did it proud and raised a glass to our benefactor.

We had had over 4,750 people in and out of the ship, including Commandos, Paras, Gunners, SBS, SAS, Fleet Air arm, Infantry, survivors, casualties, Chinese and prisoners plus our resident Electronic Warfare, Bomb Disposal Team and Mine Countermeasures Teams. We acted as an LPD, helicopter carrier, aircraft carrier (albeit only once when a Harrier had to land because the shore landing pad was out of action) and Fuel & Stores ship. We were used as a casualty and survivor reception, a special forces base for fire fighting and repair of damaged ships, as a ferry and mine hunter, Exocet decoy, electronic warfare base, alternate headquarters, troop

Loading fresh meat onto a helicopter. This was given by a farmer after we had made good Argentinian damage.

transport, bomb decoy, prison ship, Civil Aid, post war clearing up operations, submarine depot ship, cleansing station, Queen's Harbourmaster and supplier of food and water. We ballasted more times in five weeks than a submarine does in a whole commission. During all this we suffered no casualties, no major breakdown; our weapons worked; food always arrived; aid was invariably given; beach unit, landing craft and helicopters continued to operate (over 300 landing craft hours and 1,000-plus deck landings); our plans worked and we were never caught out. Everyone on board responded cheerfully and without complaint, as one, to whatever new or extraordinary demand was made of the ship.

Now at last we were on the way home. This was for real, the conflict was over, *Intrepid* had come through the experience with honour, and I personally was enormously proud of the ship's officers and crew.

After an uneventful journey home, just before we reached the mustering point outside Plymouth, the Bridge spotted a Type 22 frigate on the horizon. As we moved nearer we saw the whole crew manning the ship, that is to say they were lined up on board and as we passed them, they raised their white caps and waved them in a wide circle, cheering Hip, Hip Hooray. This was a very special moment, made the more poignant by the fact that my brother was Captain of the ship, and this was his wonderful way of saying, 'Welcome home!'

In Plymouth we unloaded the ship, prior to making a spectacular entry in the official fleet return at Portsmouth the next day. While we were in the Falklands, the Commodore Amphibious Warfare was on board *Fearless,* thus she had been the senior ship. With the Commodore out of the equation, that is off the ship, *Intrepid* would be the senior ship, as I was a more senior Captain than the Captain of *Fearless.* We had both left the Falklands at different times and had not seen each other since, but I did know that the Commodore was no longer on board. All my ship's company were determined that *Intrepid* should lead the way into harbour. It seemed to be the only thing that mattered to them.

As we came up to our mustering point we saw *Fearless* hovering on the horizon. My Commander lifted an eyebrow and asked: 'What are we going to do, Sir? We can't follow her.' I'd thought about this and replied, 'send them this message,' adding, 'Form 1.' This means form column in order of seniority, a well known naval signal. *Fearless* duly formed up astern of us and we went into Portsmouth with *Intrepid* leading a satisfied ship's company.

After our return from the Falklands in July 1982, there was a spectacular parade through London on 12 October, ending at the Guildhall. Subsequently, the City put on a magnificent lunch for the senior military personnel and the Prime Minister.

At the reception before lunch, I was to meet a man who was to become a very good friend. He was on the Court of the Livery and had been told by them to go and get a "hero". He came up to me at the reception, introduced himself and then asked me if I would do his Livery the very great honour of becoming a Livery man of the Coach Makers and the Coach Harness Makers. Well I couldn't say no, but I'm not sure they got a hero. It was indeed, a very great honour for me, and I treasure the moment they made the offer.

I was also honoured to be awarded the Distinguished Service Order (DSO) and include the citation that accompanied it as I feel it belongs to all who served aboard *Intrepid* during the conflict in the South Atlantic.

Peter and Faith outside Buckingham Palace.

Citation

HMS INTREPID, under the command of Captain Peter Dingemans, was manned up and sailed at very short notice to join the Amphibious Force already on its way to the Falkland Islands. Captain Dingemans achieved all this in a remarkably short time and joined the main Amphibious Forces at Ascension Island and stayed as a vital part of it, with the exception of one brief respite, until the Fall of Stanley.

During the time of the landings, when the Amphibious Force was in San Carlos Water, the ship came repeatedly under air attack. HMS INTREPID was, on several occasions, employed on nightly escorted runs to insert or recover landing craft when the threat of attack from the airborne Exocet and surface craft was ever present.

Throughout this period, Captain Dingemans took the closest personal charge of his Ship's Company, fought his ship magnificently, as well as providing every possible assistance to Frigates, aircraft and landing ships. His example, energy and leadership were of the highest order.

I leave the last words of this chapter, to these extracts from the speech made by the then Prime Minister, Mrs Margaret Thatcher, paying tribute to 1,250 Falklands veterans whom she saluted as the bravest and most professional Armed Forces in the world, at a champagne luncheon at the Guildhall on 18/10/1982.

'This was one of the most brilliant military achievements in modern times a triumph of endeavour and skill, planning and imagination. We owe that triumph to the best and most professional armed services. We thank you all those that are here and many more for reasons of space that can't be here.'

'The 777 valiant young men who were wounded and 255 who gave their lives and whose memory will be honoured forever, we grieve for them and think especially of their families and their sorrow...'

'In those anxious months the spectacle of bold young Britons fighting for great principles and a just cause, lifted the nation. Throughout the land our people were inspired doubts and hesitation were replaced by confidence and pride that our younger generation too could write a glorious chapter in the history of liberty...'

'We, the British people, are proud of what has been done, proud of these heroic pages in our island story, proud to be here today to salute the task force...'

Chapter 19

CREW'S STORIES

These are some personal memories from a variety of *Intrepid*'s ship's company and some from those who passed through the ship. Written in their own words, they have kindly allowed me to include them in my book, I am honoured to do so, as the Falklands Conflict is their story, as much as mine.

Mike Quinn: Steward

"In spring of '82 I was based at the Weapons Engineering School of *HMS Collingwood*, working in the Wardroom (Officers Mess). I was supposed to serve there for two years as my shore draft, after recently completing two years at sea aboard *HMS Bristol*.

Whilst aboard *Bristol* in 1981, there were two visiting Argentine Type 42 Destroyers, *Hercules* and *Santisima Trinidad,* identical to the *Sheffield* and *Coventry,* alongside Portsmouth's Fountain Lake Jetty. I regularly walked passed these ships when going about the dockyard.

In early 1982, *Collingwood* was host to a number of trainee officers from Chile and Argentina. It was customary for the Royal Navy to train foreign navies, and it was my job to look after them when they came to the Wardroom. The two groups never mixed and we, the staff at the time, did not realise the political tension between the two countries.

The course ended around February and the students returned home. I have often wondered if these same officers were involved, or knew in advance what was going to happen a few weeks later. At this time, our staff was looking forward to Easter leave and, being a training establishment, Easter leave period would last a number of weeks. Leave periods required that a skeleton crew remain behind and, whilst looking forward to leave, I was constantly being badgered by my mate Paul King to put in a request to stay behind and have a bit of a laugh manning the officer's bar and doing no good. We would then be entitled to second leave, meaning that we were not doing normal duties for around five weeks. A great plan I thought, so I made the classic mistake of volunteering myself.

The plan came together our team being Petty Officer Johnny Morton, Leading Head Paul Thomas and Andy Goodman known as Benny. The establishment went into leave mode, when news came in that Argentina had landed some men on South Georgia, and then later launched a full scale invasion of Port Stanley.

The Royal Marines of Port Stanley were ordered to lay down their arms by the Governor, to save further loss of life. I had known many marines and I knew this would only have been done in the direst situation. I knew the Falklands would only be saved by a shooting war.

The following five days were frantic in Portsmouth as the order to assemble a Task Force came through. That weekend, the streets and the area around the dockyard were crammed with military vehicles, and at night the sky was an orange colour from the dockyard lights. Monday morning the big ships sailed, whilst we watched TV.

We worked out a little planned routine; things were going well, doing as little as possible, whilst having crafty pints at the officer's expense in the Wardroom bar, and getting food from their galley. The previous Sunday, I had made my regular phone call home to Mum: 'No Mum, I'm not going to the Falklands, I'm on shore base, and I've done my sea time!' Next morning, whilst cleaning the Wardroom carpet, my world fell apart and my life flashed before me as Paul King came marching up to me and said, 'Get your kit bag, Mickey, you're going to the Falklands.' A rush of adrenalin hit me and I went straight to the heads.

Our quarter was ordered to report to the Manpower Allocation Office (MACO). It was staffed by the Navy police, or Reggies as we knew them. Time to tidy up a bit, check our haircuts and boots, but as we went into the office, the Reggies stopped, looked at us and were falling over themselves to be helpful. They said, in tones of unheard of gentleness, 'Join *Intrepid* in the dockyard lads, transport arranged for the morning; just take your steaming kit.'

I went ashore in the afternoon into Fareham to the bank. The lady over the counter looked at me and said, 'Are you going to the Falklands?' 'Yes,' I replied.

A look of motherly concern came over her, and I walked out of there like a condemned man.

I rang home for the second time; my Mum knew before a word was said that I was going 'Down South'.

Transport arranged, we arrived at Pompey dockyard to *Intrepid*, our new home; she was lying in dry dock and covered in scaffolding, pipes and orange paint. How the hell is this ship going to get anywhere, we thought? But wc knew it was going to happen and got to work straight away. The lads on board were really friendly and, whilst my loyalties were still with my old ship *Bristol*, this lot was a great bunch of lads. The ship was rapidly put back together, the old ship's company from her previous commission had been reassembled, and our *Collingwood* gaps were there to fill the gaps in our department.

My last night ashore, I had a few pints in Pompey, and on my taxi ride back, the driver said, 'Which ship you want mate?' '*Intrepid*, please', I replied. He answered in a cocky fashion, 'She going south is she? Never make it that old rust bucket won't mate, sure she won't.'

I said firmly, 'She will,' and at that moment my heart and soul were *Intrepid*'s, the 'Old Showboat.'

So there you have it, after volunteering for an easy few weeks' work, I now found myself heading for the other end of the world, to war. I was off, on the biggest adventure and the best and worst time of my life."

Mick Magin: Assistant Catering Assistant

"As an assistant catering accountant I had just joined *HMS Tartar* on my 18th birthday for a month's loan. I was based in *HMS Dryad* and had recently been given my first full sea draft to *HMS Intrepid* for the April of 1980.

Whilst in Gibraltar with *Tartar*, I was informed that *Intrepid* was coming in. After finishing for the day, I took the opportunity to go on board to introduce myself. How little did I understand then how much she was going to mean to me in the years to come.

In the April I duly joined the ship, she was due to set sail for the Med. The first issue was to find a mess that had some bunks free, as the normal caterer's mess in 3C1 was full. There was no choice but to place me in 3N mess with the Fleet Air Arm when the 845 squadron joined the ship. We stored ship and I was working initially in the fridges and freezers, six decks down in the echo section. I had never seen so much meat and veg in all my life and I thought the lifts we used would never stop.

We eventually stored the food and I got a call from the chief caterer to come to the catering office. Up six decks to the office where the Chief Beard asked me to take over the dry stores.... I was puzzled, if not a little put out, as I had just got the freezers ready for sea. I found my way to the dry stores, down another six decks to foxtrot section and down the longest ladder in the world. I had a couple of safety nets, just in case. I opened the dry stores door to be confronted by a wall of dry food, which was all over the place and piled to the ceiling. The guy who stored it could not cope with the incoming speed too readily and just threw the stuff in.

I went back to the catering office for a whinge but to no avail, I was going to have to manage one way or another. My first '1082' white list[1] came in and after four hours of searching I had to relay to the chief that I could not find a lot of the ingredients on the list. My chief, though sympathetic, told me to go back down until I found everything on the list. After several more hours I came up exhausted and informed him I had only made my way through about ten feet of the stores and most of the food was now outside the storeroom. That's when the chief came down to look for himself. I guess he did not appreciate how bad the situation was.

'Change of plan, Mickey,' he said. 'You tell me what you can see and we'll compose the menu to that.'

Thank goodness I thought, actually, it's not repeatable what I thought! So that was that. For my first trip, for the first one or two weeks the menu was derived from what was visible in the stores. I recall being about five weeks in when I declared that I had crawled my way to the top of the food to find a way to the back of the store.

I had a great time on the ship. It was not until the West Indies trip in 1981 that I eventually got to the right Mess, having spent the autumn trip in 2C barracks with the booties. I spent time in loads of foreign places, Egypt, Israel, West Indies, most of the Med, most Scandinavian countries and a trip into the Arctic Circle with the embarked force where the shutter of my SLR camera went up and didn't come down due to the severe weather, minus-40 at some stages. The Middies were with us on most jollies. I recall the West Indies especially when I saw some guys with the worst sunburn ever. The blisters looked like tennis balls hanging off their skin.

But all good things come to an end. I had given in my 18-month notice whilst on board. I was pleased with my time in the mob, especially *Intrepid* but wanted to start to settle down in London. With 12 months to go my next draft came through and I could not believe my luck. My posting was to the land-based establishment *HMS President* in Kensington, London. Thank you, Drafty! I would get a living allowance and get to live at home a lot sooner than I had planned.

Intrepid was decommissioning, a victim of defence cuts, and we all started to leave one by one. I recall vividly leaving *Intrepid* with moist eyes, but with a sense of a new beginning in the next chapter of my life with Christine while in London. Of course, there was a good knees up and the usual 'Roll on my F**king Time' (ROMFT) talk from me. So it was a bitter sweet experience leaving the ship but I was looking forward to my leave, or so I thought.

By the time two weeks later came, I had already popped into the catering office at *HMS President* to introduce myself, had a quick tour from the caterer on duty, who informed me of all the cushy routines I would have to follow. Then just at the end of my leave, I got a call from the regulating office of *HMS Intrepid*.

'Get yourself back to *Intrepid*,' the voice on the telephone barked.

'I can't, I've left her,' I answered.

'We have it that you don't join *President* until next week,' they replied.

'Yes, but I've left *Intrepid*,' I countered.

'Not until you've joined *President*, sonny. Get your arse back here for Monday morning we're restoring the ship,' was the final word as he hung up.

The Falkland Islands had been invaded and we were gathering a Task Force to deal with it. *Intrepid* had been de-commissioned de-stored and de-ammunitioned.

Foolishly I thought I would be safe as I had already left the ship. Not impressed I dragged myself with a heavy heart to Waterloo on the Sunday night and boarded a train to Portsmouth.

Intrepid was re-commissioned and needed to be re-stored and re-ammunitioned. She was to be the final piece in the Task Force jigsaw, as *Fearless* and other ships were already on their way.

No problem this time getting into 3C1 Mess, in fact my top pit was vacant. This was obviously the start of the recall process. So, miserably, I drew my curtain and went to sleep. Next morning I awoke to hear a lot of sniggering and a gasp of: 'You're joking? And replies of, 'No, he's really here!'

I opened one eye as someone lifted my curtain.

'Hello, mate, what was that you said? You won't see me again!' More laughter ensued. I, however, was not seeing the funny side of it.

I reported to Chief Caterer Bath, who seemed really pleased to see me. My face must have told a different story, because I started to whinge for what must have seemed like hours. Finally, the Chief had had enough. 'We're going to see the Commander,' he said firmly. That shut me up.

The Commander was great. He obviously realised I was not happy but gave it to me straight. He told me that I had a job to do; I was expected to do it well and without complaint. That was fair enough, I supposed. No more time for whingeing.

We had so much food to store we clearly did not have enough space in the fridges, freezers and store rooms, so we had to improvise. I think it was the Commander who came up with the idea. We made artificial walkways with the boxes. They were laid on the floor in such a way that made the floor some nine inches higher. Or, looking at it another way, the ceiling was nine inches lower. Didn't bother me, I'm only 5ft 7in but I am sure some people were developing permanent cricks in the neck.

We did well. I recall the landing at San Carlos, I also recall the only time I went up top and this was to deliver a pot mess to the guys on the Bridge and to those firing the Sea Cats, Bofors and machine guns. Up we struggled with this pot mess, lots of stairs and the food kept spilling, but we got there just as an air raid started.

'Cates, don't move!' was the shout when the machine guns and Bofors went into action. It was truly deafening and very frightening. Needless to say, when this air raid was over, I went back to running the junior rate's dining hall. It was no fun down there either.

We knew the Argies had no night flying capability, so one night we were out of Bomb Alley, no doubt taking some troops somewhere, on what is called an insertion, when an air raid warning sounded. We all looked at each other as we did not think this was possible. The skipper announced that there were two super Entendard fighters closing. My memory seems to recall that it was 40 miles and closing. I stayed next to the sink thinking (falsely) that it would give me some protection if the inevitable happened.

'30 miles. Stand by!' came over the speaker.

This was real, we had no major defences with us, we were a sitting duck. Some guy behind me started counting down 30, 29, 28. Needless to say he shut up quickly with the assistance of someone's boot. This was mad; we could do nothing about it until we had a stroke of luck. We sailed into a snow storm and they passed us by. I'll never forget that night.

We were the lucky ones; many did not make it back. Oh, my, but what a welcome when we did return. It was my father's birthday, 14 July 1982. Christine and my parents turned up to welcome us back on Fountain Lake Jetty. I was on duty on the day (in order to make sure I got the weekend off, and I did the rota. Well, call it a perk). I was in my 8's[2] so I missed Procedure Alpha[3]. We were warned that morning by the Second in Command that we would never experience another welcome like it. And he was not wrong. One of the guys came looking for me as we approached and told me there was a whacking (he didn't use that word!) great big banner out there with my name on it. And as true as you like he was right. What a welcome!

I saw my time out in the Navy on *Intrepid*. I recently went back when she was in Liverpool for breaking up. She had changed in some areas, the hatches certainly seemed smaller. I braved the darkness and visited the fridges and freezers, but couldn't summon up the courage of tackling the longest ladder in the world, in the dark."

Andy Goodman

"During the Falklands campaign, we had the Welsh Guards on board after the Bluff Cove disaster. The unharmed ones were dispersed around the mess decks, the walking wounded were put up in the Wardroom ante room. As part of the first aid party, I was detailed to chat to them while they waited to be medically attended. One Guardsman I was chatting to had both hands very badly burned; all we could do for him was apply zinc cream on his hands and put them in plastic bags. He wanted to smoke, so I lit one for him putting it in his mouth, he then said he wanted to use the toilet, so I took him to the senior rates heads. Not thinking, I waited outside. His head popped round the corner and he asked if I could help him. The penny still didn't drop. I stood there asking how I could help, he just looked at his hands. At that point I realised what I had to do. I don't know who was the more embarrassed, him or me.

On our way home, we had a fundraising night for *HMS Fearless* Foxtrot 4[4]. Our radio station was playing certain music which people had donated money to hear, while others were donating money to remove certain songs from the air.

Our mess suggested that if we donated £100 to the fund we might get the officers to serve us dinner in the wardroom, rather than us serve them. I went to speak to the Commander and he said it was a good idea but only if we donated £200, so digging deep we raised that. About 15 minutes later, the guy on the radio said that the cooks had been in touch and would only cook this meal if the amount raised reached £400. We managed this and the meal was served a few days later.

We wore borrowed officer's uniforms and they wore our half blues. Loads of piss was taken and dished out. Someone took a couple of photos and, to my great surprise when we visited Admiral Dingemans' house at an *Intrepid* re-union, there was one of these photos in pride of place entitled: *Wardroom staff being served by officers.* And there I was, grinning like an idiot, in the middle of it."

Chief Petty Officer Denby: Operations Department Co-ordinator
"I joined *HMS Intrepid* in September 1981 as the Operations Department Co-ordinator. We were in the Mediterranean with the Dartmouth Training Squadron on board and after a three-month tour we returned home for Christmas leave and an uncertain future. In January 1982 the government decided to decommission many naval ships and both LPDs, *Intrepid* and *Fearless,* were to be taken out of service immediately. This would involve a rundown period and the disbanding of the ship's company. At the time Argentina was making fresh claims to the Falkland Islands. The British government dilly-dallied and the rest is history.

I had been drafted from *Intrepid* and was on leave when I heard the news that a Task Force was being assembled. Later that day, my recall instructions were delivered by hand. The following day I returned on board to my old job as the Ops Department Co-ordinator. I was given a brief by the First Lieutenant and, on completion, I carried on to the Routine Office and started work. Over the next two or three weeks we managed to re-establish almost all of the ship's company. It was extremely important for the morale of the ship's company to have Captain Dingemans back on board. Departments were working at full throttle almost 24 hours a day, it was hectic. With a full complement now on board and having stored and ammunitioned the ship, we sailed for a four-day work-up period in the Portland area. We completed the work-up on Friday afternoon and leave was granted from 16.00 until 23.30 on Sunday night (a difficult one). I managed to get home on Saturday. When it was time to leave, I said what I had to say, then my father-in law, who was visiting me at the time transported me to the Gosport ferry (Portsmouth side). I told him that *Intrepid* would be sailing for the Falklands but insisted he keep it to himself; as far as my wife was concerned the ship would be exercising off Gibraltar (which was partially true) and returning home on completion (she has never forgiven me for this). I waved goodbye and caught the last ferry across. The bus for Portland was leaving from the Gosport side.

The following morning, with all the uncertainty and expectations surrounding our departure, the mighty *Intrepid* sailed for the Ascension Islands, en route to the

Southern Ocean. On passage we continued to train weapon crews and Ops Room personnel at every opportunity. The ship was teeming with embarked Forces, vehicles, ammunition and stores. It was a remarkable achievement to get the ship ready in what little time we had; nevertheless, there was a considerable amount of work to be done and our attitude was absolutely right.

The ship reached the Ascension Islands in good spirits and anchored off-shore. During our short stay we were supplied with more stores and equipment and one rating had to return home. Within 36 hours we were ready to sail. We weighed anchor and continued on passage to the South Atlantic. As we made our way further south the weather became progressively worse. As expected the Argentine reconnaissance aircraft had begun carrying out probing runs to within a 120 miles of the group; a submarine periscope had also been spotted astern of the ship. We had been in Defence Watches since leaving the Ascension Islands and were rapidly approaching the target zone; on several occasions it had been necessary to take the ship to Action Stations and our state of readiness was improving fast. One important task would be the transfer of embarked Forces to the LPDs in mid ocean. Meanwhile talks were continuing in an attempt to end the dispute between the British government and Argentina.

Preparations for the proposed landings had been progressed, but there was a set-back when a Sea King helicopter transporting Special Forces from *Hermes* to *Intrepid* had gone down mid Atlantic. This was a terrible moment. The Ops Room had picked up a beacon signal, but there was no word from Flyco or Lieutenant Commander Air (LCA), which caused considerable anxiety for Command. An immediate explanation was required as to why Flyco had not reacted to the beacon signal. An air search for the helicopter got underway but, unfortunately, it was found upside down with the cab totally submerged. We launched the LCVP's crew to recover what they could. As far as I can remember there may have been a few survivors.

The Task Force was now in position approx 250 miles north east of the Falklands Islands; we were fully prepared and ready to go, but there was still no news from Northwood. At the eleventh hour, word reached us that the diplomatic effort had failed. This was a defining moment and it was now inevitable that we would have to retake the Falklands by force. We accepted our lot, hoisted the battle ensign and, after a short but positive brief by Captain Dingemans, the good ship *Intrepid* altered course and commenced her run to the Falkland Islands. This was it!

In the early hours of the following morning, more than 20 warships, including the two assault ships and a number of merchant vessels, slipped into Falkland Sound. It was eerie. By 09.00 that morning the first phase of the assault was well underway. Would the Argentine Air Force respond? We didn't have long to wait.

On the first day on the landings there were 72 air raids reported over LAAWC. Things were happening very quickly, time seemed to stand still, the ship was running on instinct and collective will, it was a case of one for all and all for one. Action crews had been closed up for almost 72 hours before breaking into modified Defence Watches. Years of training was being put to the test. As the conflict developed, the possibility that we might be bombed at night was very real. Whilst at anchor in San Carlos Water, the threat from enemy divers was ever present. On more than one occasion LCVP crews, shot at what they thought was an Argentine diver, but was in fact a black plastic gash bag now full of bullets. It has never been confirmed but I was told that a 400lb bomb did actually hit the stern of *Intrepid* below the water line in San Carlos Water, but it failed to detonate.

It took the ship's company four to five days to settle down after the initial onslaught. The younger members of the ship did exceptionally well; they gained in confidence very quickly, took charge and got on with it. When the Argentine air force tried to attack units in San Carlos Water, weapons crew made it very difficult for them; they were forced to run the gauntlet, which wasn't easy by any means. On several occasions enemy aircraft flew so close that Flight Deck personnel threw nuts and bolts at them. Upper Deck crews had to endure freezing temperatures over long periods but never complained.

At anchor in Falkland Sound we knew when 'T Bone Steaks' were mentioned it meant that the ship would almost certainly be carrying out a night insertion. These planned manoeuvres, designed as a means of delivering troops for specific objectives were not exactly popular with the ship's company, nevertheless they were essential to operations.

Approximately 150 miles east of the Falklands there was an area known as the Rest Zone. As far as I remember we were invited to take some time out for a rest and recuperation. I wasn't too happy about leaving our position, we were an important platform carrying out essential tasks, why take time out? We left San Carlos Water and headed for the rest zone. On passage we located the main body and continued in an easterly direction until the following morning. Things weren't going exactly to plan. At one point we came under attack from air-launched Exocet and there was a submarine threat. After 24 hours or so we were, quite unexpectedly, told to make our way back to San Carlos Water unescorted by frigates or destroyers. As directed, we broke away from the main body and altered course for the Falkland Islands. It was broad daylight, we were on our own and more than 100 miles from our destination. This was extremely dangerous and definitely caused a sense of humour failure all round.

During the campaign the ship was closed up for hours on end but our defences were solid; staying awake for extended periods wasn't too much of a problem, one survived on adrenalin, Action Messing and plenty of tomato soup. Our endurance was tested to the full, and on several occasions I thought that our time had come, but we came through with flying colours."

Bob Lane: Former CCMech (ME)[5]

"3 April 1982. 'Return to your ship immediately.' The note like many similar that day had been pushed through my letterbox by the Naval Patrol, Portsmouth. The ship was *HMS Intrepid* which had been languishing at 5 Berth in Portsmouth naval base for months as the MoD pondered her future. There were few left on board and those of us in the Engine Rooms even fewer. Together with my opposite number, CPO 'Mo' Morris, we had decided to maintain our respective machinery space as best we could on the limited resources available. His area being the After Machinery Space (AMS) and mine being the Forward Machinery Space (FMS). One beneficial result of this policy was that we both had a good understanding of the outstanding defects and maintenance.

Mo and I were amongst the several hundred regulars who crewed the LPDs, as such we tended to serve in this same class for unusually long periods. I had joined in 1981 (and went on to stay until 1985) and had developed an encyclopaedic knowledge of the propulsion machinery, having also served for 18 months on *Intrepid*'s sister ship *Fearless*.

Both ships had a similar operational pattern for several years, primarily as training vessels in the Dartmouth Training Squadron (DTS). This involved training the future Naval Officer Corps, giving them seagoing and on board experience of a warship at sea. Though interspersed with amphibious exercises these were not frequent; a fact that assumed greater relevance in 1982. The operating pattern was not unpleasant, with termly alterations between Scandinavian and German ports and the Mediterranean. Occasionally, the cycle involved visiting the West Indies and the USA.

Several days in a port was followed by two or three weeks at sea. This did mean the Engine Room crews were kept busy, especially after arrival in port. There were two primary reasons for this: *Intrepid* had no auxiliary boilers and was fitted with diesel generators as well as steam heating and galley services. The shut down crew was also heavily engaged, since the design of the *Intrepid's* steam system meant shut down of the steam plant was followed by many leaks from the steam glands. These were of necessity positioned upside down in the machinery spaces; water gathered at the steam gland/valve spindle interface and when cooling caused leaks. The Engine Room crew would usually spend one or two days repacking these glands with asbestos packing. The net result was that the Engine Room crews got less leave than most other members of the ship's company.

Social cohesion was ensured by the bulk of ME[6] CPOs and others being messed together in the large accommodation mess 01J. We, in turn joined with other messes to form the 'Fleet and Chief Petty Officers Mess' – also known as 'the pub in the sky' by virtue of its height above sea level on 02 deck.

Collectively, the whole thing came together in that the *Intrepid* was crewed by people who knew each other and their ship very well. The machinery was reliable, though hard work to maintain, and the design was such that we were reasonably confident that *Intrepid* could do what she was designed for in wartime, offset only by the relatively slow speed and poor defence capability. All these factors and more were to be tested in the conflict of 1982.

On returning on board in response to the naval patrol recall, Mo and I held a quick conference and decided to start reassembling machinery we had dismantled for maintenance. Our concerns at the scale of this task, with a very small Engine Room contingent, were heightened when an ashen-faced officer raced up the gangway to ask, 'How quickly can you get this ship's machinery ready for sea?' Our consensus was ten days with massive spares and dockyard support.

There then occurred something we had never, in our long careers, experienced before – we got both the spares and the support. The latter in the form of a Portsmouth dockyard officer asking for a list of every defect which he and his colleagues rapidly and effectively started to deal with.

Equally rapidly, as if by magic, the original crew started to reappear, including some of those who thought their naval careers were behind them. It was about ten days later that the engines were back in steam and the frantic build-up of people and stores was reaching its climax. Sometime during this period our Captain, Peter Dingemans RN, returned on board. I knew this since as I worked in the forward Engine Room to prepare for sea, he appeared, surveyed the chaotic disarray that the machinery was in, and asked, 'Chief, do you think we can ever make it?' The answer was yes, simply because allied to the care we had taken with our machinery during the dormant period, we were receiving superb support from ashore, in our efforts to bring the ship alive again.

By virtue of my branch and location in the ship I had had little occasion to meet Captain Dingemans, during our previous sea time together. We did once meet during a famous ship's 'garden fete' held on board when, together with Kev Smith, a fellow CPO, I had organised a 'gronk board contest'. These boards, located in every mess deck, contained photographs of the sailors' current and ex-girlfriends in various stages of undress and indignity. Kev and I (known as R D Eviate and Mr P Ervert respectively) arranged a grand competition to determine who had the most outstanding gronk board in the ship. We asked Captain Dingemans to judge this and award a prize of a dozen cases of beer and a plaque with a harridan's face on it to the winning mess. He was clearly taken aback by some of the images on display, but consoled by the fact that in charging to see our gallery we raised a considerable sum for charity.

We had however discussed our Captain in 01J mess on occasion; the general consensus was that he was a gentleman in every sense of the word, who tempered the need to get the military or administrative task completed, with an obvious and genuine care and concern for the ship's company. This became even more evident in the conflict of 1982.

Intrepid sailed for the Falklands with mooted ceremony. Many of us left behind families, in my case a heavily pregnant wife with three other children, the eldest of whom was in intensive care following a potentially crippling fall and we were also due to move house in the near future. The passage south was a busy, at times frantic, continuation of the preparations for war. Our machinery performed well, its simplicity and basically sound design fulfilling its purpose and promise, to drive the ship into action.

My personal highlights of this conflict:

The exhilaration of seeing the Task Force ships in convoy all around us as we approached Ascension Island. The surprise that no radar aerials were rotating 'lest the enemy detect us'.

The clear and very dark night the SAS helicopter crashed. Bringing back memories for me of service in *HMS Victorious* in the 1960s when we scoured the sea looking for survivors after several aircraft crashes. Years later, I went to see the SAS memorial window to this Falklands tragedy set near the font I was christened in, at St Martin's Church, Hereford.

The sheer terror invoked by the thought of mines – men laid on three mattresses in the hope that the explosive shock would be dampened.

Guardsmen saying, 'It's alright for you blokes in British Rail,' as they queued to embark on to the LCVs, many of them seemingly unaware there was a fighting force called the Royal Navy.

Opening the Tank Deck door on the night of the assault in San Carlos Bay. The blue door illuminating the hold, causing hundreds of eyes to look up. The troops lined up to board the landing craft, their faces covered in camouflage, the tension palpable and the throb of the landing craft diesel engines making an unforgettable sight and sound.

Watching the SBS sergeant, who I knew from previous exercises, counting out only green tracer fire that way everyone would know when it was he that was firing. Talking to another SBS NCO the night before he was killed and remembering he said he 'was getting too old for this'.

Being with a stoker who, on enquiring, was told by an adjacent Royal Marine that the 'landing lights' he could see on the approaching aircraft were gun flashes.

Running out of sweets (nutty) early. However, we had in the Royal Auxiliary Stores (RAS) some quarter of a million tomatoes. Issued three times a day, they eventually had an adverse effect on both morale and digestion.

Body bags being disembarked from a helicopter; the RC chaplain earning his pay.

After a somewhat excitable predecessor, the Captain taking over on the action. The Broadcasts; his calm voice the epitome of leadership in action and greatly appreciated by those of us down below. A recording of one of these occasions survives and clearly demonstrates this.

The fear engendered by air attack and the chefs playing on this by dropping a pile of trays behind the PO chef, thus shattering his tranquility for several days.

The professionalism of the Special Forces not diminished by one of them being clearly frightened whilst under air attack whilst on board. The thought of being enclosed in a metal box surrounded by ammunition and fuel was, he told me, the most frightening experience of his life.

Casualties being treated in our dining hall sometimes whilst we ate our only cooked meal at midnight. Rumours especially the ones about Argentine nuclear or chemical weapons which led to a spate of gas mask thefts.

Intrepid with hundreds of soldiers and sailors on board being ordered to enter well into enemy controlled areas at night in order to land a small force of soldiers and marines. The natural harbour having enemy artillery on it. Our captain carrying out this task, made the more difficult but, from our perspective, completely right decision to land them at the earliest opportunity and avoid the risk of losing his ship; and the profoundly bad effect this would have had on the battle.

Being moved out of our action mess to make room for the Parachute Regiment – then out of the fan chamber we (the 12-man damage control team) were squatting in – then being squeezed in the corner of the passageway for weeks.

Krill wriggling and nipping, some going down my overalls, as I scooped them out of the Engine Room sea water filters. There were thousands of them shoaling around the ship's bottom, their bodies stinking out the Engine Room as they rotted; although, that said, some found them delicious as a snack.

The fear engendered when working in a steam propulsion machinery space, eight decks down, when under air attack.

The Royal Marine sergeant who, during an air attack and whilst in automotive mode, fired his heavy machine gun, located inside a wooden chacon, to exhaustion. No one having the nerve to tell him the aircraft had departed. This resulted in him putting the only known bullet in *Intrepid*.

The smell of humanity en masse coming from the ventilation system, after we embarked hundreds of Argentine prisoners of war at the surrender. Their eyes looking up when I opened the Tank Deck door just as our troops had looked up on the night of the landing.

Beethoven's Pastoral Symphony the first music I listened to in three months at the war's end.

On the way home our Captain entering the Fleet and CPO to applause, the men standing in respect for a good and caring man who had captained his ship well.

Home: our Captain rightly insisting (to *Fearless*) that we lead the way into Portsmouth Harbour and a tumultuous welcome.

My family: my wife having moved house and resolved all problems whilst nine months pregnant.

The Disposal: Accepting the *HMS Intrepid* (and *Fearless*) in my new role, as Disposal and Reserve Ships Officer, 20 years after the war.

Working on her sale to a Liverpool based ship breaker and watching the final demolition for recycling her.

The quiet moments on board *Intrepid* whilst I had her in my custody remembering.

Finally, discovering the following quotation, pinned next to the Captain's desk which I found just before *Intrepid* departed for final disposal.

'*War is a perpetual conflict with the unexpected, so that it is impossible to prescribe beforehand for all the circumstances that might arise.*

Possess in a marked degree initiative, resource, determination and a fearlessness of responsibility'."

Paul Hutchinson: Wardroom Steward

"It was March 1982. I was at *HMS Pembroke* Chatham when a strange buzz went around the camp that some Argies had invaded one of our islands and we were going to send a Task Force to sort it out.

I thought I wouldn't be going. I'd never been on a ship so I would be no use. I was only 17 years old, and my mate Dixie told me we were going on leave so they wouldn't send us. How wrong I was.

I left camp and got a taxi to Stroud, Kent to visit my girlfriend and her family before going on to my parents in Grimsby. That same night, after some food, the knock on the door came. A police officer stated that I had to go back to Pembroke and report to the gate house: 'You are so in trouble. You said you were going to Grimsby.'

Well, off I went and I reported to the gatehouse.

I reported to a CPO and, after a ticking off for not going straight to my parents, I was sent to the sick bay. After what seemed like a thousand questions and a lot of injections I was sent to the stores to draw my tropics and anything else I needed at the time. I was told to join the ship called *HMS Intrepid,* report to the Quarter Master (QM) by 14.00 hours the next day. A rail warrant was shoved in my hand and off I went. I didn't know what was happening, and I had been sent to Portsmouth to join a ship I knew nothing about.

As I entered the dockyard and headed for Fountain Lake Jetty, I saw a great grey monster with a gangway with the words *HMS Intrepid* and I knew I had arrived. I rushed up the gangplank to be greeted by the QM. I still remember his words (I wish I knew his name) 'What's the hurry son?' he said. I gave my apologies for being late and explained I had to join *Intrepid* as it was going to the Falklands. The QM told me to leave my kit bag at the gangway and took me to the Bridge, explaining that the ship had been scrapped. I looked around and could see the Bridge was empty. I gave him my joining papers and he took me to 3K2 mess deck which was also bare. The QM said, 'Pick a bunk, you're the only one here, and if this tug goes to war I'll get you a case of beer.' He then left as I picked a locker and, a bunk and within hours, more and more people joined with the same story. 'We are going to war!'

Well, we know the rest. The trip to the South Atlantic left me with sunstroke on the way there, fear and sea sickness while we were down there and a great sense of having grown up whilst on the way home. On 14 July 1982, two days before my 18th birthday, we arrived back in Portsmouth. A large crowd of people were waving banners as our *Intrepid* took station ahead of *HMS Fearless*. I looked out at the mass of people on the dockside and I saw my parents amongst them. I was so proud to be part of that crew that sailed on such a fine ship, and I knew we would be shipmates for the rest of our lives."

Able Seaman Neil Wilkinson: Gunner

"It was dark when we entered San Carlos Sound 21 May 1982. I remember the day like it was yesterday.

We had sailed from Portsmouth at the back end of April and had headed south to join the remaining part of the amphibious force at Ascension Island. It had taken over two weeks to catch up with the Task Force as it headed south and it took a further ten days to reach the Sound.

I was only 22 years old and had not long been in the navy. I was drafted to *HMS Intrepid* in early 1980, straight from the gunnery school and after her decommission in 1981 I was told that I would be joining *HMS Sheffield,* later hit and sunk. Luckily, when *Intrepid* was recommisioned to go with the Task Force they reinstated as many of the original crew as possible. I had joined to see the world and be paid for it. It had never occurred to me that one day I would be in the theatre of war.

The mood on board was changing as we reached the Ascension Islands. There were still idiots who thought that it was brave to spout off in front of everyone. This, of course, is the worst thing you can do, and I preferred to keep my thoughts a little reserved.

It is fine in an exercise when you are using dummy ammo, dummy drills and even aircraft that buzz you and fly off, but this was going to be the first taste of action for the Royal Navy in a very long time.

The journey south seemed to take ages, the weather didn't help and we suddenly went from virtually no clothing on the equator to wearing wool jumpers and thermal clothing.

The briefings were very much on capabilities and when we would be closed up at action stations. We already knew what to expect as we had had a full run down on what they had.

It still didn't sink in that in a few days' time we would be in full battle. The mood was definitely changing though as we crept closer and closer to the islands. We knew we weren't getting turned round and sent back home, this was it!

The lower decks by this time were like an ant's nest that had the top removed. People moving about with weapons making ready; the nerves beginning to jangle slightly. We had to carry respirators, flak jackets and foul weather equipment.

We had on thermals, two or three pairs of socks, gloves, anti flash hoods and gloves, and when we got to the upper deck we then had helmets and radio headphones.

The ammunition was laid along the side of the Bridge wings, still in their cases, four clips of four shells in each box, all greased up and ready to load and fire. They were greased because of the weather, and when firing a lot of ammo through the gun it kept the barrel well greased and protected from the weather.

My mood altered, I was now finding myself as their leader, I was the aimer and in charge, imposed but never the less it was there.

It was pitch black outside, we had the odd flicker of a torch light on the ship, this was in red lighting, the odd person would walk by, you couldn't tell who it was, only by their voice.

My main concern was something that had never bothered me before, but suddenly did. The breach of my gun was on my right, which meant my vision was impaired by the breach, so my reaction time would be less, unless I did something about it. I had only a 90 degree firing arc, so I turned the gun from facing forward to facing the full 90 degrees, this way I could see anything that flew into the area. On the port side they had a 90 degree arc, but because their arc was to the left of them they saw a lot more that was coming our way.

So I decided that most of the time my gun would be pointing straight out across the side of the ship.

The *Belgrano* sinking was a bit of a mystery, some said it was sailing towards us, then another different tale would pop up. All we knew really was it had gone to the bottom.

The *Sheffield* sinking was a reality check for me; it had been going to be my next ship, the actual ship I was due to join after I had left *Intrepid* on decommissioning.

All I could think was, would it have been me, would I have been on her when she was hit?

I suppose when it's one of your own ships you get a different feeling. I'm not saying that the loss of life on the *Belgrano* wasn't bad, and I suppose it's very difficult to explain this one, but the feeling is different.

As we eventually got closer to the islands, the threat from the aircraft carrier was gone, due to the sinking of the *Belgrano*. This did not mean aircraft could not attack us as they could reach us from land or use inflight re-fuelling so we had to be on our toes.

As we entered the San Carlos Sound early that morning all was quiet. There was nothing but the noise of our ship and the dozens of other ships around us, all hidden by darkness. I expected some sort of action being so close to land, we all did. None came. Not then, anyway.

We had been at action stations since late the night before and we were still closed up for the morning watch, which meant I was at my action station as light broke over the Falkland Islands. As I looked out over the gun sights I could see the lines of the mountains as they silhouetted against the dawn sky, and I knew that this was going to be a difficult day.

Disembarkation of the hundreds of Royal Marines, troops and equipment began almost immediately. We were now sitting ducks, unlike some of the frigates that sailed up and down the Sound putting a protective cordon around us. We had ballasted down to allow the landing craft to enter and exit the dock and, as such, we could not move more than a few feet here or there.

As the morning drew on, the threat of attack from the air grew more and more imminent. The first attack came shortly after 10am. Luckily most of the land forces had been disembarked but we still had a lot of 3 Para on board and if we got hit a lot of men would certainly die. That first day in San Carlos was long and tiring with repeated air attack and several of the escort vessels being hit by bombs. Fortunately many of the bombs had not exploded on impact, a factor that saved many lives that day and in days to come.

I wrote letters home (still have them, too) to my Mum and family. I recall the first one was after nearly 32 hours closed up at our weapons and we were told we could stand down as the threat of night attack was minimal. I found a quiet lock up, near the gun, and sat down to write my letter. This was going to be a bit like my last letter home, only because of what I had seen and witnessed throughout those hours.

The writing was small because of tiredness and I usually didn't do sloppy letters, but this time I told them how I felt and said that I didn't think I would be coming home after what I had seen. Then I sealed the letter up, reflected on the day that I had just witnessed, then began to cry myself to sleep.

The emotion was far greater than I could ever describe. Here I was, thousands of miles from home, fighting to save my friends and protect my ship, even myself, to retake a distant land. It was all too much. I eventually fell asleep, possibly a few hours sleep, maybe less but much needed. It was not long before we were told to stand to again. Sleep was much disturbed in San Carlos Water.

We soon began to expect the air raids and we joked and drank hot tea while we waited. As anticipated, the air raids would come and I would fire off my 40mm shells at them as they flew down the Sound and out of sight.

On the 23 May I fired a salvo of rounds at one of many aircraft attacking the ships in the Sound. I fired off a five shot burst hitting a Mirage that had only minutes earlier dropped a bomb on *HMS Antelope*. As I watched I saw a tracer hit the aircraft just behind the cockpit, blowing off the wing and tail section. The aircraft disappeared out of sight before crashing. *HMS Antelope* later exploded and sank.

27 May was initially a quiet day. No air attacks, not until later in the day when two Skyhawk aircraft slipped into the Sound unnoticed by the guard ships.

I was sitting near my gun doing a word search puzzle when all hell broke loose. The two Skyhawks had managed to fly into San Carlos and drop a few bombs; nobody knew they were there, not until the sound of the jet engines could be heard roaring up the Sound towards us.

We had all been in an unprepared state of readiness, my gun crews were around but not in the area of the gun. I immediately leapt to the gun and fired off six rounds at the aircraft as they flashed by. I saw one shell explode very near the second aircraft but was not sure if I had scored a kill.

It was weeks later that I met John Knott, the Defence Secretary at the time. He had asked me if I hit anything. Before I had time to answer, the Captain, Peter Dingemans, stepped forward and replied for me. 'Two aircraft, confirmed kills,' he announced proudly to the Secretary. I was proud of my actions and gave the Secretary a satisfied smile.

Since then 25 years have gone and I have often thought of the two pilots that I shot down. I knew the first one had been picked up and had survived the crash but what of the second? At the time we were enemies but as time moved on, so had my thoughts towards the pilot and his family. I began to wonder what had been his fate and how it had affected his family and friends.

I started to do some research and one night, while at home watching a TV documentary about the war, I was hit with the realisation that the second pilot had survived the crash. He was there on my TV talking to the presenter of the documentary, telling how he came to be shot down. He was recounting the day, May 27 explaining in Spanish how he and his wingman had slipped into the Sound and had attempted to bomb the ships. The sound of the pilot's voice was almost inaudible over the presenter translation, of his story but I hung on to every word.

I knew straight away that this was the man I shot down all those years ago. How did I know? Well on the 27 May only two aircraft came into San Carlos, one went back to Argentina, one didn't.

It was simple deduction and, from that point on, I knew that I had to find the pilot. It took me eight months but I eventually found him. I am happy to say we are now in communication via e-mail and I hope to actually meet him face to face in the future.

Some people may ask why I am doing this and may criticise me for wanting to do this. To those people I say, we are no longer enemies. At the time both of us had jobs to do. I had to live with the belief for over 25 years that I had killed the pilot. To see him alive on television lifted that burden."

Private Clive Jeffries: Royal Army Medical Corps Private

"In 1982 I was a 19-year-old private and had been a soldier for just over a year when my unit (16 Field Ambulance) was tasked to sail with 5 Infantry Brigade to the Falklands.

The majority of the unit left Southampton on the QE2; I, however, left a week later with the rear party. We flew from Brize Norton on a VC10 via Dakar, Senegal to Ascension Island. This was my first realisation that this was a serious business when I saw the Vulcan bomber being prepared for a mission.

After spending a few hours plane spotting we boarded the Fisheries Protection vessel *HMS Dumbarton Castle*, which carried about 100 soldiers of various units on deck, with the intention of transferring them to the *QE2* as she passed Ascension. Prior to this, my experience of being at sea was confined to crossing the Channel on a ferry.

It was quite exciting as we got under way; we were over flown by helicopters and saw a low pass by a Nimrod.

We were at sea for about six hours. I sat by the bow enjoying the pitching of the vessel and the flying fish jumping out of the bow wave. With growing excitement I saw the *QE2*, the *Dumbarton Castle* slowed and we were prepared to cross deck by Sea King helicopter. This was when I felt seasick and threw up on the deck, much to the annoyance of a sailor who would probably have to clean up. I then got my first helicopter ride.

We landed on the *QE2* and were met by the RSM who directed us to our quite comfortable accommodation. The next week was spent training and exploring this impressive ship. We then arrived at Cumberland Bay, South Georgia and saw the Argentine submarine *Santa Fe* badly damaged alongside the jetty at Gritviken. Our CO managed to get ashore and visit Shackleton's grave.

We then transferred from the *QE2* to the *Norland* ferry and along with the seasick Gurkhas, we set sail for the Falklands. About a day into the journey it was announced that we were entering the exclusion zone, so the next air raid warning signal would not be a drill. After three days *Norland* arrived at San Carlos Water on 1 June.

The unit was landed by LCU at Ajax Bay, to be told we were in the wrong location, so we went to the San Carlos settlement, where we spent a week living in fire trenches or crammed into the community hall. During this time I witnessed an Argentine Dagger aircraft shot down by one of the frigates in San Carlos Water. There were numerous air raids. It was cold and wet and miserable but our morale was still high as we waited for the inevitable move forward.

It came as a relief when on June 7 we boarded *RFA Sir Galahad,* and the relative comfort and warmth of the ship, with hot food from the mess rather than a mess tin and ration pack. I remember having a lovely night's sleep in a comfortable bunk in one of the accommodation compartments on the port side.

In the morning I remember being shown the area near the bow where there was a compartment damaged by a bomb the previous week in San Carlos.

I went up on deck. It was a sunny day and I could see *Sir Tristram* that had arrived the previous night anchored nearby. I heard later that the ridge behind Fitzroy had been shelled by Argentine artillery shortly before we arrived.

There was no sense of immediate danger; we had breakfast, then lunch, even got to see some movies on a projector in the mess, courtesy of the crew. I made my way back to the accommodation and saw the Welsh Guards preparing to disembark. Many of my unit were already ashore, leaving only about 30 of us medics with our 21c still aboard. I went through to the Tank Deck and stopped to talk to two of my unit. I cut short my conversation because I needed a pee. I then went back to my port side accommodation where my kit was, as I knew we would be leaving soon. I had just lain down on my bunk when an air raid Red was called.

It only seemed a few seconds later when even down below I could hear the roar of a jet overhead, quickly followed by a loud thud and a whooshing noise, and felt the ship move.

I was still unsure what had happened, so I and about ten others in the compartment waited for instructions. They came after about five minutes, when I heard what you don't expect to hear as a soldier: 'Abandon ship!'

This is when it dawned on me that it was probably quite serious. We made our way up the stairs to a passageway that runs parallel to the Tank Deck, looking towards the stern which was now on fire, smoke filling the passageway. You could feel the heat coming from the hatchway leading to the Tank Deck. I saw a man on fire through this smoke before he fell over. There did not seem to be a way out.

I went from complacency to thinking I was going to die here in the space of ten minutes. Looking back, I am bewildered about how calm I and my comrades were, except for one who started screaming we were going to die. He was punched in the face by one of my friends and that seemed to calm him down.

Then, as if by a miracle, we could see daylight coming through one of the hatchways. It was the area damaged by the unexploded bombs from the previous week. A damaged hatchway that had been covered by a tarpaulin had been opened leading to the deck above. The ladder had the first ten rungs or so missing so climbing up was very difficult. I managed to climb out and helped the others get on to the ladder. We could see the life rafts full of men already launched drifting away from the ship. I then made my way to the upper deck of the bow. I remember thinking, 'Holy Shit!' when I got there. The Bridge was completely alight and there were secondary explosions. A Chinese member of the crew was manning a hose by the bow; I remember thinking that it was a bit futile with the scale of the fire confronting him.

There did not seem to be many people left on board by this time. Helicopters were overhead but seemed to be finding it difficult to hover over the bow. I saw terribly burnt men, some without limbs, being winched up.

Some members of the field hospital had set up on the forecastle. We went there, but were told to get off the ship as soon as possible; it was time we were all leaving, as the worst casualties had been evacuated.

A corporal who had obviously not just escaped from down below like us suggested we go back down to the Tank Deck and see if there was anyone we could rescue. He was told to 'F**k off'.

I saw two or three men jump over the side. We all had lifejackets and could see the shore a few hundred yards away. I can swim that, I thought. I was just about to follow them when an officer grabbed me by the scruff of the neck and advised me in a robust manner that I would die of cold before I got to shore.

It was then we saw a Mexefloat come alongside. Luckily for them it had picked up the men who had jumped. I then climbed over the side down a scramble net, with about 30 of the soldiers still on board. This was probably just in time, as the deck was getting so hot my boots were starting to melt.

On the Mexefloat one of my unit fell into the water and was pulled out by me and others just before he was squashed between the float and the side of the ship.

Ammunition was exploding, something pierced the hull and flew under us. It was time to leave.

No one said a word as the Mexefloat pulled away slowly from *Sir Galahad*. I will never forget that view of the ship, which by now was burning out of control. The Mexefloat travelled round the headland and I could see that the helicopters were no longer hovering above it. I couldn't help wondering if anyone was on board; if so they would have little chance of escape. We were so lucky. The Mexefloat arrived at Port Pleasant close to Fitzroy.

I made my way to the settlement and went into the community hall being used as a makeshift aid post. I was not prepared for the sight and smell of burnt men laid out on stretchers. This was too much for me; I went into shock and went outside again.

There were casualties everywhere; helicopters were landing taking them up and then flying them to the field hospital at Ajax Bay and other ships. There were many men wandering around in a daze, some crying. I composed myself when confronted with a group of the Chinese crew walking up from the beach. Most of them seemed to have burnt hands. I located a hose in the outbuilding, as they all seemed to gather round me, so I started using this hose to cool down their burns.

After a while everything seemed to quieten down and some order was restored, when another air raid came. An Argentine Skyhawk came in low followed by a tirade of small arms fire from the Infantry (2 Para) dug in on a ridge behind Fitzroy. I just stood there watching. You could see the white helmet of the pilot as he flew overhead dodging his aircraft from side to side.

There was even the bizarre sight of one of the cooks from 5 Brigade HQ firing his weapon from the hip, swearing as he ran down the field after it. I later learnt that many of 21C and two other members of the Royal Army Medical Corps (RAMC) were killed. They were the two I had been talking to on the Tank Deck before going for a pee. This probably saved my life.

Sometime later I was evacuated by Sea King; sitting by the door gunner I rather enjoyed the ride, very exciting. He landed on *HMS Intrepid*. The crew was very kind to us, we were provided with a hot meal and a warm bunk but no one slept that night, the events of the day running over and over in our heads.

The next day I helped in the sick bay taking the wounded up to the Helicopter Deck. I recall helping a man still able to walk but blinded by the flash burns to his face. A Wessex landed and I helped him walk slowly to the aircraft. We were nearly there when a seemingly uninjured sailor ran past us and the loadmaster signaled for us to go back to the hander, the person who controls who goes on the helicopter, as they were now full. So slowly and painfully we went back.

This is when I think the shock hit me. I got very angry about this and became abusive, losing all composure. I was ordered below to calm down.

Later that day, I was taken by LCU with others to Ajax Bay where Rick Jolly, the Senior Medical Officer, explained that we would not be going home but would now be put to work. Some of my unit thought that the war was over for them and got quite irate, as documented in Jolly's book, *The Red and Green Life Machine*. I feel this is an unfair account to the majority of us, as we just quietly got on with it.

I spent the remainder of the conflict assisting mostly Argentine casualties.

The day after the ceasefire, I was repatriated to my unit at Fitzroy where I spent a month before being moved to Port Stanley, then on to the hospital ship *Uganda* in her new role as a troop ship. We set sail for home, along with the Gurkhas, a few days later."

Lieutenant P Ingham – PWO (Principal Warfare Officer)
"Our arrival in the Falkland Sound/San Carlos Water area took place on a bitterly cold, damp morning. There was little wind and sound travelled far, which, combined with a Gun Direction Platform's crew brief on the possibility of bombardment, or small arms fire from ashore, ensured that all were extremely attentive to even the smallest change in detail.

With known enemy troops in the area we were, therefore, relieved and somewhat surprised to arrive at our initial allocated anchorage in the Falkland Sound unmolested. To the West of us, shortly after anchoring, Naval Gunfire Support commenced in the vicinity of Pebble Island and continued until first light, the skyline being lit up like a fireworks display. At this stage it all seemed a little distant and unreal. It was not until just after first light, when the ship had shifted anchor berth into San Carlos Water, that the fireworks were to start for us.

Just after the 12.15 action snack, the first enemy air activity in our vicinity was detected. Then came our first visual acquisition half a wing of a PUCARA was seen to show above the hill on our Port Quarter and the 40/60 opened fire against this target before it dropped behind the hill, attempting to attack the troops ashore. This first sighting, fortunately, set the adrenalin flowing in all the upper deck crews, keying us up for the attacks which were to materialise later in the afternoon. There were many tense cries of 'Alarm Aircraft!' as a bird took to the air on a distant hill, only to be discounted as the supposedly fast moving target went into a hover. The main events of the afternoon were to be attacks made by A4 and Mirage aircraft. Compared with peacetime practice, the immediate thing that comes to mind was the sheer speed and determination of the attacking aircraft. Alarm procedures were just fast enough to bring the weapons to bear and, more often than not, one was looking down on a passing aircraft from the Gun Deck Platform (GDP). The pattern of attacks of this afternoon was one where the aircraft made their approach up and along the Falkland Sound, attacking ships in the Sound en route, then making a hard right hand turn into San Carlos Water where they proceeded to attack the amphibious shipping involved in the off-load.

Our first raid that afternoon was Mirages entering from the Sound attempting to attack *SS Canberra* and *HMS Antrim* who were on our port beam. This was a good raid for us because the Port Forward Sea Cat was fired, giving us a chance to overcome the butterflies everyone was feeling deep down, before we became the target.

It was interesting to note that, once the nerves were calmed after the first couple of raids, to a man nobody took cover during the air raids as they were far too busy urging each other on to take out the aircraft. Positively jumping up and down at times! This first raid was also a great confidence booster because we saw one Mirage turn away and one pilot eject, as a direct result of Sea Cat fired by ourselves and *HMS Plymouth*. She turned out to be a trusted friend over the forthcoming days and Warfare Officers from *HMS Broadsword* told me that to see aircraft approaching either *HMS Intrepid* or *HMS Plymouth* was a delight, as we both seemed to fire at anything with everything at the drop of a hat. This policy of lead before accuracy seemed to work and, whilst it was very difficult for any one ship to claim responsibility for destruction of individual aircraft, we seemed to be able to deter them from greater things.

The air activity was continuous throughout the afternoon but there was no worse moment than when, with one air raid crossing the ship's head from left to right dropping a pattern of bombs 100 feet on the port bow, another aircraft, a Mirage, appeared out of nowhere over the hilltop on our starboard side and closed fast. We had that gut feeling that success was his for the taking and time literally stood still. The starboard Sea Cat fired and, for what seemed like an age, the aircraft kept coming with the Sea Cat closing. Luckily, before releasing his bombs or firing at us, he eventually turned hard right and literally fell out of the sky behind a hill for cover, and I suspect he ditched his bomb load since he did not appear to re-attack. This was one to us, and from then on the confidence and effectiveness of *HMS Intrepid*'s weapons crew took a definite upward turn. The afternoon continued in a haze of air attacks with little time to collect one's thoughts before the next alarm indication. By dusk all involved were exhausted and it was a great relief when darkness fell. The Argentines only had a limited night flying capability.

The second day saw us at Action Stations at first light, for a day which proved to be an anti-climax compared with the previous day's activities. The Argentines were obviously taking stock of damage sustained so far. The only raid was at dusk, by two A4 Skyhawks, which proved to be ineffective as the weather conditions were against them and it was obviously based on the previous day's anchorage positions which had been changed overnight. Had they remained the same, *HMS Intrepid* would almost certainly have been hit.

The third day almost came as light relief with attacks mainly by A4s. A lucky day for us, as bombs fell short by 100 feet and, in the heat of battle, spent Sea Cats from another ship managed to straddle us – fortunately no damage was done. Talking of own goals or penalties, it was also not uncommon for 4.5 inch shells from our ships defending themselves to travel over the hill from the Falkland Sound into Bomb Alley (San Carlos Water) though no one was hit. However, handicaps apart, this was the last day in which the Argentines were at liberty to attack with little hazard, as the Rapier batteries were not fully established ashore, and they made the most of their opportunity. After a forenoon attack, when the A4s were so close they might have been Airwork Hunters doing a fly past at the end of a tracking serial, the afternoon became less awe inspiring.

One particular raid of A4s and Mirage were seen to cross the bay ahead of *HMS Intrepid* as a Mirage passed over *HMS Antelope*, clipping the top of the mainmast and bending it, before it burst into a burning mass of metal and crashed into the sea. This was as a result of a Seawolf hit by *HMS Broadsword* but not before the aircraft had laid an unexploded pattern of bombs on *HMS Antelope*. Unfortunately one of these bombs was to explode that night and *HMS Antelope* became a raging inferno, a reminder to us all that the Argentines were a force to be reckoned with. During this particular afternoon raid the Commander on the Bridge will never forget watching through his binoculars one enemy pilot literally pedalling his aircraft through the wall of fire until our starboard Bofor took off his wing tip and he disappeared over the hillside.

Another evening, later that week, saw a daring raid by Argentina on Red and Blue Beaches at last light, when they accurately bombed our ammunition supplies, causing many casualties. This was an impressive performance because the A4s came in very low and managed to avoid detection until they were actually in San Carlos Water, *HMS Fearless* was the first to spot them but they had successfully fulfilled their role. However, it is with some satisfaction that *HMS Intrepid* can claim to have hit both these aircraft with 40/60. The sympathetic explosions ashore were to go on long into the night.

The whole situation in San Carlos Water is best summed up by a well known phrase in *HMS Intrepid*, 'Keep a good look out and watch out for the low bogey.'

JT Shepherd: Rehabilitation Co-ordinator

CPO Shepherd produced this helpful guidance to assist with rehabilitation:

"Dear Parent/wife/girlfriend/neighbour/friend/acquaintance,

Once again the peace and tranquility of your home and neighbourhood is going to be interrupted by the arrival of your son/spouse/lover/next doors' terror/friend.

Upon his arrival you may notice that your once good looking, suave, sophisticated, lazy, drunken sailor, has undergone a transformation and is now nothing more than a shadow of the person he once was. DO NOT worry, for I am sure with a little love and affection (something which has been missing whilst he's been away), we can restore him to the lively person he was before he went away to fight for his country.

Below are a few guidelines which, if adhered to, should ensure complete rehabilitation within a matter of weeks.

Upon his arrival greet him as normal, be sure to show him that you love and care about him and tell him how much you have missed him. This will make him feel wanted again. Try not to show a look of surprise if, when you meet, he is wearing long white evening gloves with a filthy white hood and a life jacket. These items are now his most treasured possessions. DO NOT, REPEAT NOT, under any circumstances try to remove these objects from his person. The effect could be disastrous on him, yourself and your home and he would feel totally naked without them and would go to great lengths to prevent you from removing them. It may take a while, but in time I am sure he will discontinue wearing these ridiculous items. It is essential he does this in his own time. Do not hurry or push him because if he feels his prize possessions are being taken away from him, he will become very aggressive and start dismantling things, mainly you and your home. YOU HAVE BEEN WARNED.

It would be advisable, before his return, to set aside one corner of the bedroom for him. Try to obtain a hard black rubber mat, preferably with lots of little grooves in it, a blanket and possibly a pillow (not essential as he would prefer to use his life jacket as a pillow), place these objects in the aforementioned corner. This should ensure that your son/spouse/lover/friend knows that you really care about him.

Do not get worried if, when night falls, he crawls into his little corner and goes to sleep fully clothed. If this does occur, wake him every three or four hours and offer him a cup of soup and a tomato, or cheese roll and tomato.

This small gesture, I assure you, will bring a radiant smile and a look of sheer delight to his lovable little face. However, if you wake him and do not have a tomato for him, he will be very upset and will probably not talk to you for a while. Try to ensure he gets a tomato with everything he eats and he should remain happy.

After a week or so try to get him to sleep in a proper bed (fully clothed at first) and start him off on stable and solid food. This may take a while as he has been sleeping on black rubber mats and eating nothing but soup, cheese/corned beef rolls and tomatoes for some time. Please be patient with him as this is a most important stage in his rehabilitation.

If your loved one smokes, do not be surprised if you notice a lapse in this habit. During his time at war, he has been conditioned to smoke only when told to do so. If you ever see him biting his fingernails and looking totally perplexed for want of a cigarette, retire to your kitchen, get hold of a plastic cup (or beaker), and return to the vicinity of where your war hero is anxiously sitting. Place the plastic cup or beaker near to your mouth and shout, 'One all round'.

This should bring immediate relief to his face and he will automatically delve into his pockets and offer everyone a cigarette. Please do not refuse this offer as it may upset him. It would be advisable to repeat the phrase 'One all round' at least once an hour to get him smoking regularly again. After a short while, he should offer to share his cigarettes without hearing 'One all round'.

We now come to what I consider as the most vital part of his rehabilitation. It is imperative you keep him out of earshot of sirens, or anything that sounds vaguely like a siren, as this could have a devastating effect on him.

If by chance he does hear a siren, he will think that he is about to come under attack from the enemy. Stay well clear of him at this time as he will be in a state of total confusion. He will, upon hearing a siren, run around in a mad frenzy trying to locate his white gloves, hood and life jacket. Upon finding them he will put them on and dive to the floor, covering his head with his arms. Once he is in this position, leave him for approx ten minutes. To return him to normal, again using a plastic cup (or beaker) to give the effect of a tannoy, shout 'AIR RAID WARNING YELLOW… RELAX ANTI FLASH'. It would be advisable to follow this with 'One all round'. He will now feel safe once more and will offer his cigarettes around. Within a few minutes he should be his normal self again and carry on as if nothing has happened.

Please try to ensure that he does not leave the security of your home until he has completed this phase of rehabilitation. I am sure you can imagine the chaos he may cause upon hearing a siren if he is out shopping. Try to remember that the public at large are unaware of his fragile condition, and are not as understanding as you; they may try to commit your loved one to an asylum if you are not careful.

My last piece of advice concerns safety of life, namely his and any member of the opposite sex he may come into contact with, before being completely rehabilitated. He has not seen a female for quite a while and the effect of seeing one will undoubtedly make blood rush to his head and other parts of his anatomy. He will do anything to get a member of the opposite sex in his clutches and to hug and kiss her. This could be very embarrassing if she is a total stranger. I therefore strongly advise you keep all females out of his reach for at least three days and then, with someone beside him, let him watch them through a door or window. When he shows he is in control of himself, very slowly start introducing him to some of your female companions. I will leave it to your judgement to determine when it is time for him to be let loose on the streets.

I hope these guidelines are of some help and assistance in the rehabilitation of your loved one. You will probably find all that is needed is love and affection blended with a little understanding. If you have any questions on the subject of rehabilitation do not hesitate to contact me. I will do my utmost to try and resolve your queries."

Michael Fleming: Leading Weapons Engineering Mechanic (Radio)

"My action stations during the Falkland conflict was on Starboard aft Sea Cat, as the console operator.

I have always told people that during the most frightening moments of conflict, the Captain's calm reassuring commentary during the raids, were instrumental in how well we fought as a ship. I was plugged into the weapons crew comms system, but could hear him talking in the background over the main broadcast from the Ops room. I have often equated it to a cricket commentary, which is a bit surreal for all that was going on around us. But it did the job. For me as a weapons console operator it gave me the confidence that we were indefatigable. Thank you."

George Heron – Leading Signalman
"My vivid memory of the Captain was his calmness in a crisis that transmitted confidence to all officers and men around him during many trials and tribulations.

I don't know if he will recall this but when two Skyhawks swerved away from *Intrepid* at the last second in San Carlos instead of carrying out their bombing run and we all froze, white knuckled, on the Bridge, he sat down in his chair and calmly, shaking his head, said, 'How odd, why did they abandon their attack?' Later, he told us over the tannoy of Harrier intervention that wasn't visible to us but was to the two Skyhawks. I will always remember his calmness throughout. And I think everyone has fond memories of his reassuring daily messages over the tannoy.

I'm in a job now where I am in charge of people and when stress levels rise I do think back on his calmness while in charge of a warship in serious waters and I do try and copy his approach to problems. And I'm sure I'm not the only ex-*Intrepid* that still does that. I'm sad to see *Intrepid* go but her legacy carries on."

Notes
1. The form on which menus were ordered.
2. The name given for working clothes.
3. The procedure under which sailors, in dress uniforms, line the decks.
4. The callsign of the landing craft from *HMS Fearless* which was sunk by enemy aircraft.
5. Chief Mechanician.
6. Marine Engineer.

END OF PART TWO

PART 3

AFTER THE BIG EVENT

Chapter 20

COMAW

On my return from the Falklands, I left *HMS Intrepid,* for the last time and, in 1983, was promoted to the rank of Commodore. My full title was Commodore Amphibious Warfare (COMAW) and The North Atlantic Treaty Organization (NATO) Commander for the UK and the Netherlands Amphibious group (COMUKNLFIBGRU).

My responsibilities were to plan, direct and exercise NATO and national amphibious operations worldwide. My experience in the Falklands conflict obviously gave me a real understanding of the difficulties faced in amphibious warfare as well as the problems in working across the services to create a harmonious approach. It was a superb opportunity to use the experience learnt on *Intrepid* in both peacetime and during the conflict. It gave my planning and my directing exercises real backbone.

In the Royal Navy an Admiral and certain other appointments such as COMAW would fly their own Flag on the ship they were using as headquarters or the base they were using ashore. This flag demonstrated that the Commodore was there, it could not be flown, unless he was there in person.

The COMAW's broad pennant was a rectangle, with a red cross and one red ball in the top left hand corner, and a fish tail-shape cutting in down the right hand side.

It was rather wonderful to have one's own flag.

In my dual role I was responsible for the training of UK amphibious forces and, in a NATO context, this remit included planning, directing and exercising the Dutch marines. We were constantly testing out the amphibious procedures. Another of my responsibilities under NATO was to reinforce northern Norway, Denmark and the Baltic approaches.

In the Exercise Cold Winter 1983 we were to test the reinforcement of the Northern Regions of NATO likely to be used in a time of tension. Forces involved were UK Amphibious Forces and US 4th Marine Amphibious Brigade.

For exercise purposes it was assumed NATO had made a rapid political decision to enable a Task Force of amphibious ships to sail and reinforce northern Norway, which was under threat from an undisclosed enemy. I had 20 ships under my command and was to rendezvous with the American Amphibious forces off the northern coast of Norway. I also had 600 bags of mail for the American forces, as they had taken a long time crossing the Atlantic.

My Task Force consisted of ships taken up from trade (STUFTs) and other UK specialist amphibious ships, such as *Sir Percival*. The American amphibious force was made up only of naval ships and they looked very smart. They could not disguise their shock and horror when they saw the motley collection of ships at my disposal. But they realised with a certain amount of shaking heads, that such a force had recently re-taken the Falklands.

As the combined forces approached the Norwegian coast, we were attacked by the Norwegian fast patrol boats at 40 knots in the guise of the enemy, and fought our way to various anchorages to disembark the Royal Marines and American marines. There was a lot of snow at the time and the amphibious ships remained at anchorages, ready to supply the land forces with ammunition, food and stores.

This joint exercise was considered a great success and I think the Americans appreciated our sharing the very real recent conflict experience we had endured in the Falklands.

*　　*　　*　　*　　*

Another exercise in 1984 called Bold Gannet, was concerned with testing operational procedures of the UK/NL/FIBGRU and the UK Mobile Force (UK Army) as well as forces from Denmark, Germany, Norway and the USA. The first phase of this exercise was a tactical deployment of these forces from the UK to Denmark.

There were general discussions in Copenhagen about the exercise and its purpose, which was designed to test as many elements as possible, in a joint amphibious assault.

The landing force consisted of 4/5 Commando (UK), the Royal Netherlands Marine Corps, Royal Fleet Auxiliaries, four Landing ships logistics, seven Stufts and 17 German LCUs.

I took this force round the Danish Isle of Bornholm and, mid circuit, changed its defensive role into one of attack as the Enemy, carrying out an opposed amphibious landing, on the mainland of Denmark.

We were monitored all the time by Soviet intelligence gatherers. As we approached the landing we were also attacked by aircraft from Germany, Denmark and Norway. It felt like San Carlos all over again.

In the event, very rough weather hindered our disembarkation, which was carried out in nearby ports. In real life or real war conditions, the weather conditions would not have prevented the disembarkation from the amphibious ships and landing from the LCUs, but safety of limb in this exercise was paramount.

*　　*　　*　　*　　*

I could not help but to bring to mind the problems I had faced when deciding to disembark the Scots Guards much further away from their chosen location than was deemed feasible by their officers. *Intrepid* made many more nightly insertions in that area, and I like to think that by making what, at the time, was a very unpopular decision, I saved the ship and crew for the sterling work they performed across the services, during and after the conflict. This experience underlined the importance for the army to have proper training and experience in amphibious warfare. Something I was determined to ensure in my current appointment.

In another exercise I flew my broad pennant in the aircraft carrier *HMS Hermes*. This was a large NATO naval exercise across the Mediterranean, but concentrated in Turkish waters.

There was a gathering of ships and senior Commanders in Constantinople for final orders, then we went to our ships or sailed them to our given positions.

On the way to our location we passed the area south of the Dardanelles, known as Gallipoli. This is an infamous name in the history books of WW1, as it was where the British, having failed to break through the Dardanelles using naval forces, now attempted to land armies at the southern tip of the Gallipoli peninsula.

Conceived as a strategic masterstroke, the Dardanelles gamble only resulted in eight months of trench warfare, and a final loss of 120,000 troops. This was a gamble that did not come off.

The landings themselves on the bloody dawn of 25 April 1917 set the high note of catastrophe and gallantry with raw young Australians and New Zealanders facing the white heat of modern warfare and falling in their hundreds on beach after beach.

This should not have surprised the combined forces Commanders. The Turks had had months to prepare their defences and the landing points chosen were beaches surrounded by high cliffs. All the Turks had to do was station gun emplacements along the cliff tops and shoot the soldiers as they landed, or were disembarking from their rowing boats.

This disaster and the men who died are remembered in Australia and New Zealand annually on ANZAC day.

As we progressed north to our exercise area, I reflected on how anyone could have been so stupid and cold blooded, to order the landings where they did. A much more suitable place would have been further north of the peninsula on the western side, which was the area we chose for our amphibious exercise.

For two hours, the forces who were to take part in a dramatic spectacle for a watching audience of NATO dignitaries, Turkish officers and several other Commanders from non NATO countries poured on to the beach by helicopter and boat. The landing was such a stylised piece of work that it has been referred to as an amphibious ballet and a good Royal Tournament display.

The arrival of the combined forces ashore had been carefully rehearsed, so that as many of the invasion force as possible would reach the beach simultaneously. The Turkish authorities had gone to a great deal of trouble to ensure that the assembled VIPs would enjoy the show as much as possible. They had built a new dirt road on the approach to the landing beach and were keeping it watered down to reduce the dust clouds. Marquees had been erected for the greater comfort of the visitors and a water supply had been installed.

The spectacle and the comfort were soon to be challenged by a heavy rain storm that passed through, destroying the newly built road and instantly dissolving the vehicle park. To add to the problems, a helicopter came into land with some more guests, blowing down the marquees which had been erected for their comfort.

Observers, trying to keep dry in the deluge, used the half flattened canvas for shelter. Never, in my experience, have so many top brass fled the scene in such disarray with, it must be admitted, nowhere to go.

There was mud everywhere, and one Admiral dressed in his best Whites fell over and was last seen scowling his way to the flooded vehicle park. Despite the discomfort of the observers, the amphibious forces conducted themselves with huge aplomb.

*   *   *   *   *

On passage to reconnoiter in the Faroes, we had an amusing lesson, in the different attitudes to mixed company in each navy. The Danish navy had a more relaxed attitude on board their ships than our own, as we were to discover.

The Commander in Chief and various other high ranking officers had been dined by the Danish navy one evening and after a very pleasant meal and a couple of whiskies, I and the Commander 3rd Commando Brigade walked down to the cabin we were sharing. There, leaning in front of our cabin door, were a couple immersed with each other and oblivious to our presence. I had no idea what to do, but the Brigadier with us walked up to them, tapped them on the shoulder and said in a loud voice: 'Roll over once!' this they did, without breaking their clinch, and we went into the cabin.

Chapter 21

GIBRALTAR

At the end of 1984, just before the Christmas break, I reported to my Admiral Flag Officer 3rd Flotilla (FOF3). I told him that all amphibious ships were secure and we could therefore go off and enjoy Christmas.

At that moment his telephone rang and the following one-sided conversation took place. 'Yes, he is here. I'll send him to a telephone... How very interesting.' He then turned to me and said, 'Peter, would you like to go downstairs to an empty office and answer this telephone call.'

As I walked into the designated office, the telephone rang and the Naval Secretary proceeded to confuse me even further. 'Peter,' he said, 'are you sitting down?' I replied, 'No, I'm standing up.' He then came back with, 'Well, sit down.' I was really worried now. Then, with a smile in his voice, the Naval Secretary said, 'You've been promoted to Admiral, and you go to Gibraltar in March.' This really

Gibraltar from the air.

silenced me, but thanking the messenger I returned to my Admiral. He greeted me with a huge grin on his face and, with great kindness, offered his congratulations.

*　　*　　*　　*　　*

As well as being Flag Officer of Gibraltar, I held a NATO appointment, Commander Gibraltar Mediterranean (COM GIB MED) and as such, I was responsible to COM NAV SOUTH in Naples, an Italian Admiral. My remit was to protect allied ships passing through the area that covered the approach to the Straits of Gibraltar from either the Atlantic or the Mediterranean. As a result, I travelled to meet my fellow NATO Commanders in Naples and Lisbon on a regular basis.

The Spanish navy was just beginning to come into the NATO fold, but the sovereignty of Gibraltar was always a problem.

This appointment allowed my wife Faith to accompany me and, in fact, her role as hostess of The Mount, our official residence, was of equal importance to my role as Flag Officer Gibraltar and Senior Officer of the Services.

It was a full time job for us both as we had to entertain the great and the good as well as any visiting dignitaries. We had staff to help us, but menus had to be created and the environment had to be welcoming.

In my first few days I had many callers, telling me what they did and how they did it. No visitor was more important than the local trade union leader Joe Bassano. The trade unions in Gibraltar had not been weakened by Margaret Thatcher as they had in the UK, so the environment was of a 1960s type; in other words, war between boss and worker.

Joe Bassano was a remarkable man, he had been sent to England to take a degree, sponsored by the TUC, and in his spare time had done every job imaginable: from candlestick maker to lorry driver.

We got on very well together and agreed that neither he nor I would leave the other in a corner, although I sometimes wondered if our agreement had slipped his mind.

On one occasion Joe rang me at The Mount with a request to talk over a particular matter. I told him to come straight up and he did so. The only problem was that we were in the middle of hosting 24 people to a grand dinner party. So I told my Chief Steward to keep on plying our guests with alcohol until we'd finished our meeting.

Joe and I sat in the study with a large whisky in our hands and he relayed the problem.

Our visitors were fascinated by this exchange as they heard a lot of laughter coming from us through the door. Rumours flew around the room: 'Was it war or peace?' Peace prevailed and Joe departed and our rather inebriated guests sat down to dinner.

*   *   *   *   *

I was pleasantly surprised when the UK-designed, land-based Exocet was sent to Gibraltar, giving me the ability to control the Straits with some real fire power. The package consisted of a control cabin, the launching platform, mobile radar and spares all on three trailers, so it could be positioned anywhere on the island.

It was based on the captured land-based Exocet first deployed by the Argentines in the Falklands conflict, and the weapon that gave us so much concern out there.

I used to deploy the system at the end of the Rock overlooking the Straits, where it could be seen by passing ships and be offered as a potential threat to them should it be necessary. I'd love to have been able to use it on the smugglers who had extraordinarily fast boats and gave us quite a few headaches keeping up with them, but my job did not involve starting WW3.

*   *   *   *   *

A rather unusual honour was granted to each new Head of Service on their arrival in Gibraltar. Gibraltar is famous for its ape colony which plays an enormous part in the tourist attractions of The Rock, and the local population has a great affection for them.

This honour was granted to Faith and me shortly after our arrival. Two newborn apes were named Peter and Faith respectively and we were granted birth certificates for each. We thought these additions to our family wonderful and had them framed and placed in the downstairs cloakroom. To be honest, we then forgot about them,

Ape birth certificate.

until one day Faith heard the following conversation from two of our guests: 'Have you seen the birth certificates downstairs?'

'No, I haven't.'

'Well, there are birth certificates for Peter and Faith hanging up and their mother is named but not their father. You'd think they'd want to keep that sort of thing to themselves.' Faith stepped in before rumours of incest or worse started the rounds.

*   *   *   *   *

My wife is a very good athlete and took up wind surfing in Gibraltar, becoming very proficient. There was a little stretch of beach at a place near the airport, nothing special, but you got wind, sea, sun and surf.

I loved the fact that Faith was enjoying this sport so much, but I did worry a little that the wind would blow her into Spanish waters and the thought of Faith being arrested by the Spanish navy did not bear thinking about. She had, however, assured me this was very unlikely.

The army battalion on The Rock had just changed over and the new young subalterns came rushing down from their barracks to make the most of this little beach and the sea and sun. One of them came swaggering down the beach, jumped on his board and yelled at the woman surfing to get out of his way. She had right of way but she let him through and continued with her sail. She told me about it when she returned home, but thought it best to let things lie. These things tend to work out in the end. Sure enough that evening Faith and I hosted a grand dinner for the new battalion, and as the subalterns made their way down the receiving line Faith nudged me, and there was the young subaltern who had been so rude. On seeing Faith he went a whiter shade of pale and was still apologising when we went into dinner.

*   *   *   *   *

My parents were coming to Gibraltar to visit us. I was thrilled that they had agreed to come, but there was one major problem. While my mother was quite happy getting on an aircraft, my 83-year-old father absolutely refused to fly.

One of the good things about being Flag Officer of Gibraltar was that you were informed of ships due to call into the port at Gibraltar. In fact, all Royal Naval ships on a seagoing passage tended to call into Gibraltar for fuel, provisions or repairs.

I discovered that a frigate was leaving Portsmouth about a week before my parents planned visit to me in Gibraltar. The ship's journey would include a visit to the dockyard and, therefore, she would be the ideal choice for my father's transport there. As a member of the RNVR my father was entitled to travel on a Royal Naval ship.

His rank at the time was Honorary Surgeon Captain and thus his name would have to be included in Daily Orders, so some might have assumed he was joining the ship as the ship's doctor.

My father loved being at sea again, and could be seen daily making a rather shaky passage along the deck, holding hard to the rail on the bulkhead.

As he passed two sailors chatting, he overheard this little exchange: 'Who's that? Is it the new doctor?' 'I hope not' the other replied, adding more forcefully, 'If it is, I'm not going to be ill on this trip!'

My father thought this hysterically funny and told the story to all who would listen.

By the end of their visit we had persuaded him to fly home. This was going to be a first, because he had never been in an aircraft before. There was a small airport in Gibraltar and British Airways had boarded all the passengers, then rang me at The Mount, my official residence, telling me they were ready for my father to arrive.

We were driven down to the airfield right up to the steps of the aircraft, in true VIP style. My mother and father boarded the aircraft and then took off to return to the UK.

With some concern, I rang them up a few hours later to see how the trip had gone. My mother, laughing, handed the phone to my father. He told me how very pleasant the experience had been and how much he had liked the pretty waitresses, who made a great fuss of him.

Chapter 22

NORTHWOOD

After my tenure in Gibraltar, a job both Faith and I adored, I was appointed as Chief of Staff to the Commander in Chief Fleet at Northwood, the Joint Force Headquarters for National Operations and Headquarters for NATO operations. My job was to run the Fleet on a daily basis on his behalf the Fleet being the whole of the seagoing Royal Navy. I reported directly to him.

The CinC was a major NATO Commander and spent much of his time visiting his NATO contemporaries in the organisation and, of course, ships of the Fleet. As a necessary consequence, I spent much of my time in the bowels of the earth receiving communications from all over the world and from every type of ship.

As I had to be on call at all times, we had to live on the Northwood base. Faith and I were provided with a residence in Northwood and staff to help run it. It was a large rambling sort of place and we entertained many visiting dignitaries and Commanding Officers visiting Northwood. This kind of hospitality was part of the job.

One evening we were hosting a party for the Air Force and they were represented by an Air Vice Marshall who asked my wife, 'Does your husband shoot?' Faith replied, 'Yes, he'd love to.'

She was referring to a conversation we had had recently about me taking up shooting. So we didn't think anything of it, until the next morning my PA came in and said that the Air Vice Marshall was on the telephone and was inviting me to a shoot at Burwood House. Would I like to go?

I considered, then decided that if I didn't take up this offer I would never do it, and so I said, 'Yes, of course.'

I then rang Holland and Holland, the famous bespoke sporting gun, rifle and sporting clothes manufacturers. They also have shooting grounds where they can teach you to use a sporting gun, and the etiquette of the shoot.

I said 'I've accepted an invitation to a shoot. Can you kit me out and show me the ropes?' adding, 'I must tell you I know nothing about it.' I went down to their shooting grounds and they were marvellous. I was kitted out with the correct clothes and I bought myself a Spanish gun, which they taught me to use effectively, as I was more used to Bofors guns. They then proceeded to inform me of shooting etiquette and the technical language I would be expected to know.

We stayed overnight and enjoyed a delicious dinner. My fellow guns included the Chief of the Defence Staff, and many other dignitaries. When I joined the shoot the next morning, Holland and Holland had ensured that, instead of being an embarrassment, I had a wonderful day's shooting and acquitted myself well and shot three birds. I carried on shooting for many years afterwards.

Chief of staff.

*　*　*　*　*

My family and I have often visited the Henley Regatta, which is held annually, hosting a huge variety of rowing teams from the UK and abroad. As Chief of Staff, if I was away from Northwood, I had to have a car with special communication systems, so that under my remit I could be alerted if anything untoward was occurring at any time or in any place.

I was returning to the car to get the traditional picnic when my bleep rang. The duty officer said there was a crisis in the Gulf. He had the Captain of a ship based out there who wanted to talk to someone urgently. I said, 'Put him on,' and he came straight through to me in a car park in Henley from the Gulf. He said, 'We think the Americans have just shot down an Airbus. I am coming to you to see if there is anything you want me to do at the moment. In the meantime, I'm heading straight to the area at top speed.'

My reply was: 'Continue to close up to the incident, but make it quite clear in your communications with the Iranians that you are on a mercy mission, not an aggressive one.' I told him he had done the right thing and to call me later and report progress.

Apparently the US ship had thought that the airbus was a missile, because there were Iranian surface craft in the vicinity, and the plane's flight path was descending towards their position, which was unusual. The first missile from the US ship took the tail and the second hit the wing. The pilot had no chance to save the plane and 290 people died.

The Airbus was in defined commercial airspace and the American government admitted liability which led to a flurry of diplomatic activity.

A strange conversation to have in a Regatta Car Park.

My three boys visited us soon after we took up residence in Northwood. As they came into the hall, my middle son James noticed a big red button just next to my desk. Ever curious he wanted to know what it was.

I said, 'My predecessor told me it doesn't work, so I didn't bother to ask what it did when it was working.' So James, who could not resist the temptation, proceeded to press the button. All hell broke loose. Screaming cars, sirens blaring, skidded to a halt outside the door and huge armed Royal Marines burst into the hall ready to protect me. So we found out what its purpose was and that it was working after all!

As Chief of Staff I ran the headquarters part of the Purple Warrior Exercise. This was set up to test all the post war improvements we had introduced after our experiences in the Falklands conflict.

It consisted of a large amphibious force going to the defence of an island, in this case Arran in Scotland, in the most lifelike scenario possible. Some of the residents of Arran volunteered to act as evacuees, in an imaginary evacuation. For the purpose of the exercise we called Arran, 'Narra'.

The BBC programme *Horizon* asked the MoD if they could film the exercise. This was approved and for five days their camera crews were allowed to record the process of military command as it occurs. It was quite unnerving to see a cameraman lying on the floor with his camera directed at your face.

I hope the programme gave the general public some idea of how the Royal Navy works with other forces and its useful peacetime role in defending the UK.

The problems with recreating the Falklands scenario was that, without a real threat of invasion or a real enemy, the local population were not suitably shaken and frightened, it was more of a game to them. This is not a criticism of the participants just how it was.

Mrs Thatcher visited Northwood to meet the national and NATO staff and their wives at a tea party. I was acting as her escort and as we were falling behind her programme, I mentioned this to the Prime Minister and suggested we speed on a bit. She turned to me with one of her well known looks, and said very quietly, 'My dear Admiral, I will tell you when to speed up.'

A chastened Admiral led his Prime Minister down to a meeting in the Operations Room and a briefing presented by a senior officer. Following this there was the normal question and answer period. A member of the audience asked a question of the presenter, at which Maggie, with an audible huff, interrupted, saying: 'He's already told us that,' adding, 'For goodness sake, pay attention.'

*   *   *   *   *

In 1987, after two years at Northwood, I was asked to call on the First Sea Lord. It was to be a rather earth shattering interview. We chatted pleasantly, then he dropped the following bombshell: 'You have done really well in this post, Peter, and contributed a lot to your area of expertise, and been an enormous tower of strength to your CinC.' He then added with a wry smile: 'I am afraid to have to tell you, Peter, that this is the end of the line for you. I have no other post to offer you and you will be retired from this post and the RN from early in the New Year.'

I was shocked by this decision and, I have to admit, rather hurt, as I felt I had completed every role I was given successfully. However, after 37 years in the Royal Navy, you learn to accept orders, and I accepted this one with, I hope, dignity and with a determined resolve to seek out new challenges in my civilian life.

I packed my desk for the last time and went round a series of 'Goodbye, Peter!' occasions. I did not regret anything, but looked forward to a new chapter and the chance to prove my abilities in a different career. I was only 54 years old.

There was certainly plenty of life in the old sea dog yet.

Chapter 23

TAKING UP NEW CHALLENGES

My professional life has continued to be fascinating. I was able to use the skills I had learnt in the RN in a series of full and part time posts, which gave me both income and inspiration. I hope my success in civilian life will inspire those in the forces facing early retirement. Don't forget you are highly trained and highly employable.

The Royal Navy offer a series of courses to retiring officers, which are meant to prepare you, for what can seem an uncertain future, after so long in one *'firm'*. I found them useful but was still pretty daunted by the prospect of finding a good job in my 50's.

Of course high ranking officers have a lot to offer, but civilian life is very different and the civilian approach differs enormously from life in the forces. On one of my first interviews for a civilian job, I arrived at the company headquarters and was sent to the Office of the Director of Appointments. There sat a lady who said in a very friendly manner. 'Good Morning Peter, how are you?'

I was flabbergasted. It turned out that she was the wife of a senior civil servant and they had come out to Gibraltar on a short trip, when I was stationed as the Flag Officer there. In my executive naval role, I always made a point of inviting visiting civil servants to stay at The Mount, which was my official residence there. In that way, it gave me the opportunity to see who they were and they could get to know me.

This Director immediately started to reminisce about the wonderful time she and her husband had had in Gibraltar and the terrific hospitality Faith and I had given them.

Then bringing herself back to the present said: 'Now about this job.' I thought this was a pretty good start to the interview

I joined Argos Asset Management (an offshoot of the Merchant Navy Officers and Ratings Pension Scheme) as Director of Administration. My job was to act as a sort of troubleshooter. In fact I was also the Compliance Officer which meant that if the firm erred in the eyes of the Bank of England or any other financial institution, my job was to conduct an inquiry and report to the board.

The top brass in the firm had been told by their auditors and others to sort out their accounts properly or they would be disqualified. This would be very bad for the company's fiscal reputation within the City. This was not a good scenario hence my appointment, as their clean pair of hands. When I arrived in my allocated office, there was an empty desk, save for a half full bottle of whisky, empty bookcases and empty filing cabinets. I was not sure at first of what I should be doing to root out any wrongdoing, but I was informed that an internal inquiry would be my first step.

I had conducted enquiries in the navy, so thought that the best approach was to conduct this one on normal naval lines, get both sides of the story and produce my report from the findings. The last witness I called was a Director who I considered, a very arrogant man.

Having conducted the inquiry, I concluded that we had made a mistake, we should have known better and we'd better hold our hands up to the Bank of England. I read out these findings to him and other members of the Board.

Returning to my office I went in and shut the door. I'd just got back to my desk when the door was flung open by the arrogant Director, who screamed at me, that I could not conduct an inquiry in this high handed manner and he was going to do something about it.

Rather stunned by this attack I told him that I had been asked to conduct an inquiry, I thought it had been conducted fairly and if he wanted to complain about my methods or conclusion, he could put a formal complaint to the Board.

He went out and slammed the door. I remained in my post so although my manner might have been a little naval for City folk, it produced the required result.

That was my introduction to the City.

*   *   *   *   *

The time for remuneration had come round. People were going to be called by the Managing Director and told what their new rate was. The MD said, 'Peter come in and watch.' I queried, 'Are you sure?' 'Yes it will be fine, just sit quietly in that chair while I interview people,' he added.

The first one came in and the MD said; 'You've done very well. I'm putting your rate up from £90,000 to £95,000.' My immediate reaction was 'Wow, that's something.'

The recipient did not have this reaction. He banged the table in front of him and shouted; 'I'm worth much more than that!' There followed a heated discussion which culminated in a raised offer of a further £10,000. It was quite an eye opener.

Come Christmas we all got a bonus as well. I'd never had one before, but I got £3,000 that year. My wife and I were delighted.

I was made redundant by Argosy Asset Management, when it was taken over by Ivory and Sime, a company which we had created and which was based in Edinburgh, and which ended up taking us over. A typical case of the child who eats its mother. However the year before, I had flown up to Edinburgh with the new Managing Director and it was decided that I would take over the Administration of both firms. He had also asked me if I knew anything about pensions. I had said I did not know a lot. He was keen for me to do this as he thought that I would be the ideal person to take over the pension side. But after a year, costs had to be cut and I was one of the victims.

I am proud to say that I left behind me an organised Pension office and at least 50 files of detailed accurate administrative information.

So, there I was, on the streets. I had a redundancy package of £10,000 and could keep my car, which was a Mercedes, and I had my naval pension, so it wasn't skid row, but it was all a bit shattering. On the journey home, I wondered if there was a bright future for a man in his 50s.

*   *   *   *   *

A few weeks later, I got a letter from a fellow ex-Director, who had also been made redundant. He very kindly enclosed an advert for a job, listed in the Accountants Journal, as he thought it might be good for me. I looked at the ad and decided it was worth a try. I rang up the number quoted and asked them if I could send in my CV.

I rang them, when I was in London for a different appointment.

'Yes, please,' they said. So off I went to the rather palatial offices of the headhunters. I reported to the reception desk and was asked to take a seat anywhere I wanted. I sat next to a large column and, as I settled down to wait, two men walked by in deep conversation.

'We've had a lot of trouble with this one,' sighed one of the men, adding, 'Now some Rear Admiral has applied.' His companion said in a positive tone, 'You could be on to a winner with someone like that.'

I have no idea who they were, just two men talking – walking past. But I kept my ears pricked for any more snippets of information and I felt slightly more at ease with the situation. Once called for the initial interview, I was pleased to see one of them was sitting on the interview panel, I knew then I had a chance.

One of the interviewers asked me if I knew that the job was for Slaughter and May, a leading international law firm. I replied 'of course'.

I got through that first interview successfully and was then sent to see the team at Slaughter and May. I was interviewed by a variety of people and passed through a great many stages. Finally I was told that I would be going to see the Senior Partner.

He reckoned that I had a pretty good track record but then with a wry smile he said, 'What about this Admiral thing?'

I replied with a similarly wry smile, 'If you want to call me Admiral, or Mr, or Peter, you can. In fact, you can call me whatever you want'. He was obviously relieved by this, but he then came in with the real bouncer. 'You're quite old aren't you?'

My heart sank, this was it, my age was going to be a problem.

Looking at me steadily he said, 'I want you to see five partners. They are all very young, in their thirties and all very bright.' So I went to see these five. The first minutes were typical banter.

Then one said, 'You were in the Falklands. What was it like down there?' I had an open goal before me and I kicked the ball straight in the net. I gave them my life and times on the good ship *HMS Intrepid* and the Falklands.

At the end of my time I asked, 'Gentlemen have you any other questions?' They all shook their heads and, shortly after, I was told that the Senior Partner and his team were happy to employ me.

There followed ten happy years as Head of Pensions Pay Benefits and Insurances. My naval training had given me a good start in administration, and without good administration even the brightest people and the best organisations cannot function.

*　*　*　*　*

On my retirement from Slaughter and May I spent three years as a strategic advisor to St Dunstan's, the home for blind servicemen. Their Chief Executive had no military background or experience but, in the past, he had been the Chief Accountant so appointment was very much – buggins turn.

Following my advice, the post of Finance Director was created and filled up by an excellent man, who ensured that St Dunstan's remained on a secure financial footing, while the staff and management continued to offer the high quality support and help to patients and those in need. It was a joy to contribute something to an organisation I so admire.

At the same time I became a trustee of the Brighton College Scholarship Fund. The role of the trustees was to attract finance to the funds and ensure the investments made by the fund were sound. My tenure lasted approximately nine years and it was a fulfilling experience, in a constantly improving educational establishment.

As is the case so often, my role as a trustee of Brighton College attracted the attention of those looking for new members of the Council for Sussex University.

I was on the Council for six years bringing my administrative skills to the world of education and resources. It was a whole new area of expertise and a great experience. The creation of Sussex Innovation Management Ltd, a university led concept which provided newly set up companies with all the backup and support they needed. We offered local accommodation with a prestigious address, in a hitech environment; there was well maintained office space, meetings rooms and conference facilities. The communication systems were perfect for the creation and growth of technology and knowledge based companies.

There was legal support, patent advice and even a good restaurant in which to entertain prospective backers or clients.

It was a great success and I thoroughly enjoyed being in at the start of this innovative programme.

I was involved with Sussex University for twelve rewarding years.

2003–2010

I smiled when I was elected a part time Governor (to represent the public) of Queen Victoria Hospital in East Grinstead. Both my late parents had medical backgrounds and I was sure they would have been proud of my new position.

For six years I wrote papers, created new administrative policies and guarded the public purse, alongside some of the best 'retired brains' I have ever worked with.

In 2007 I was nominated a trustee of the pension fund at Slaughter and May. It meant that I was elected by the membership, and as I knew the company and the personnel well, I think I was a suitable candidate. I thoroughly enjoyed the position and the meetings gave me a fascinating insight to the continued workings of a great institution.

In 2010 I decided it was time to retire again. This was partially due to my increasing debility caused by Parkinson's Disease. I had been diagnosed with this in 1996.

I believe that I am testament to the fact that it does not have to stop you doing great or small things with your life, but it obviously, by its very nature, curtails many activities and professional practices. My new found love of shooting was the first casualty.

Without the support of my wife Faith and her insistence that I get on with my life as normally as possible, I would not have been able to do half the things I have since my retirement from the Navy. I look forward now to my new role as author, yet another turn of the page and one I hope you have enjoyed reading as much as I have enjoyed writing it.

The pull of *Intrepid* still lingers on, something I discovered when going into hospital for a hip operation.

After the operation, as I came round into recovery, a 'voice' said to me 'You'll be alright Captain.'

I would have shot out of bed, but I couldn't move anything. Very few people called me Captain, as those in the forces knew I was an Admiral and civilians tended to call me Mr.

The 'voice' explained that he was a male nurse in charge of the recovery room. He had served in the Falklands. 'In fact,' confirmed the voice, 'I was on your ship *HMS Intrepid* in the Falklands, Sir.'

At that time *Intrepid* was acting as a clearing station. People were coming to board and we'd give them immediate first aid, and depending on their injuries, they were taken out to *SS Uganda,* the hospital ship or sent to other bases. We thought that rather than just have a lot of nurses meeting the injured as they came on board with their terrible burns, we would also appoint a sailor to each one. Our premise being that they could talk about some interest they might have in common and, we hoped, they would feel less intimidated and it would help the shock factor. The doctors fully supported this move and I think it really did seem to ease the terrible suffering so many of them were experiencing.

My 'voice' had been in the medical service all his service life and was serving as a medical nurse on *RFA Sir Galahad* in San Carlos Bay. He was slightly wounded when it was bombed and was airlifted onto *HMS Intrepid.*

(Clive Jeffries tells his own story in the Crew's Stories Chapter 19)

My 'voice' told me about his transfer to the hospital ship *Uganda* and his subsequent rise up in the service, which he left in due course. So here he was now nursing me, and as if that was not enough he added a little more support. 'Don't worry, Sir. If you can't find me, there is another man here from *HMS Fearless.*'

Indeed, I give thanks to the wide naval net.

THE END

ABOUT THE AUTHOR

Peter Dingemans was born in Steyning, West Sussex in 1935 the eldest of five children. Educated at Brighton College, he entered the Royal Navy in 1953.

He became an expert in Torpedo and Anti-submarine warfare, and acquired specialist experience of amphibious operations.

As Captain Fishery Protection he was responsible for policing the extended economic zone to 200 miles.

He attended both the Royal Air Force staff course and the Royal College of Defence Studies. His commands include Her Majesty's ships *Maxton*, *Berwick*, *Lowestoft* and *Intrepid*.

On 4 April 1982 his instructions were to take *HMS Intrepid* out of reserve and to join the rest of the Falklands Task Force waiting on Ascension Island. The retaking of the Falkland Islands by HM Armed Forces was an incredible achievement. This book is about the training and experience given by the Royal Navy to Peter Dingemans which allowed him to command and fight *HMS Intrepid* so successfully in the Falklands Conflict.

On return from the Falklands he was appointed Commodore Amphibious Warfare and took charge of the national and Dutch amphibious forces. He was then promoted Rear Admiral and appointed as Flag Officer Gibraltar. He held the NATO appointment as COM GIB MED (Commander of NATO forces in Gibraltar and that part of the Mediterranean adjoining Gibraltar). His final appointment was Chief of Staff to the Commander in Chief Fleet in Northwood.

After retiring from the Royal Navy he worked in administration for 10 years in the City, first for Argosy Asset Management company and then for Slaughter and May. He has served on the Council for Sussex University, been a strategic adviser for St Dunstan's charity, Governor of Queen Victoria hospital in East Grinstead, and a member of the Council of Brighton College. He and his wife Faith have been married for over 50 years, and they have 3 sons and 10 grandchildren.

INDEX

Index Note. Subheadings dealing with biographical elements or events of war are listed chronologically.

A

Acapulco, 35-6
active rudders, 67
Aden, 57
Alexandria, 100-101
Algeria, 9-10, 46-7
America *see* United States of America
Amsterdam, 61-2
Antigua, 32
appointment selection process, 78-9
Argentine forces
    aircraft and aircraft attacks, *130,* 130-33,
        140-41, *147,* 181-3: pilot shot down
        by *Intrepid*'s gunner, 176-7
    Exocet, *116-17,* 140, 145
    navy, 116-17, 174-5
    surrendered soldiers, 151-2
Argos Asset Management, 201-3
Ascension Island, 110, 117-18

B

Bahamas, 26-7
Bangkok, 55, 71: Queen Victoria's statue, 73
Bassano, Joe, (Gibraltan trade unionist), 193
Belgrano, 116, 174-5
Bermuda, 22, 26, 32
Bodmin Moor camp, *63,* 64
bofors, *132*
boilers, 60-61, 62*n*
Bold Gannet, 189
Bombay, 54
Borneo, 72
Bracknell, RAF Royal Airforce Staff course,
    74
Brazil, 30-31

Brighton College Scholarship Fund, 204
British Army, 37, 42-3
    5th Infantry Brigade, 143
    Chieftain Tanks, *96*
    Ghurka Rifles, 143
    joint exercises, 42-3, *96*
    Parachute Regiment (2 Para), 115-16,
        139, 143: (3 Para), 139
    Royal Army Medical Corps, 177-80
    Royal Marine Band, 23, 30, 34, 49
    Royal Marines, 90
        3 Commando Brigade, 137-8, 151
        42 Commando, 139-40
        45 Commando, 139
    Sandhurst Royal Military Academy, 37
    Scots Guards, 144, 145-6
    Special Air Service (SAS), 138
    Welsh Guards 1st Battalion, 143-4, 150
British Broadcasting Corporation (BBC), 200
Buccaneer plane, *68*
Burwood House, 197-8

C

Canada, 35
Ceylonese navy, 54
Channel, 86-7
Chiefs of Staff, 90-91
Chilean Navy, 28
Clapp, Commodore, 120, 138
Clyde Regatta Week, 81
cod wars, 82, 85-8
Colours, 61
Court of the Livery, 156-7
Crossing The Line ceremony, 27
Cuba, 22-3
Cyprus Patrol, 49-53: *HMS Maxton*
    collision, 65-7
Cyprus, British Army Base, 89-90